My Weekly Sidrah

Melanie Berman & Joel Lurie Grishaver

Torah Aura Productions
Los Angeles

USING MY WEEKLY SIDRAH

My Weekly Sidrah is designed to involve your young students in the cycle of the weekly Torah readings, and to help them establish a regular habit of Torah study. We hope you will find the book straightforward and easy to use. Here are a few suggestions to help you get the maximum benefit from the material.

1. If possible, set up a regular routine for studying *My Weekly Sidrah.* You may wish to synchronize your lesson with the sidrah read in the synagogue during the same week. You can get the schedule of sidrot from a standard Jewish calendar or from your synagogue bulletin.

2. While the narrative summary of each sidrah is designed for young children, the language will probably be too difficult for independent reading, particularly at the beginning of the school year. You will most likely read this section to your class, having your students follow along in the text. You may wish to list key words and names on the blackboard or experience chant to expand sight vocabulary.

3. Once the instructions are explained, most of your students should be able to complete the exercises for each sidrah by themselves. While the children are working, you may wish to circulate through the class to provide support and encouragement.

4. The quotations provide an authentic piece of Torah text as a stimulus for discussion and future learning. Encourage your students to derive meaning form the text, and create an atmosphere in which they feel comfortable sharing their opinions. There are many "right" answers.

5. The comments are designed to promote a personal involvement and connection to the events in the sidrah. Some of your students may feel more comfortable sharing their comments in small groups rather than in front of the whole class. Furthermore, while some students may be able to write down their comments, others may need help. This is a wonderful opportunity to involve a student assistant or a helping parent as a part of a teaching team, working as a scribe with a small group. As an alternative, students could finish the activities or color in the pictures while you spend a few intimate moments with each group. Once the comments are recorded, you may ask a number of students to share their responses with the class.

6. You are not expected to finish the book! We have deliberately included all 54 of the sidrot so that students will be introduced to the entire Torah cycle. Hopefully, the students will take the books home with them at the conclusion of the school year and continue the weekly Torah habit with they parents, building upon the foundation you have established during the school year.

ISBN 0-933873-21-2
©1986 Torah Aura Productions
Torah Aura Productions
4423 Fruitland Avenue
Los Angeles, California 90058
Manufactured in the United States of America.

Bereshit

בראשית

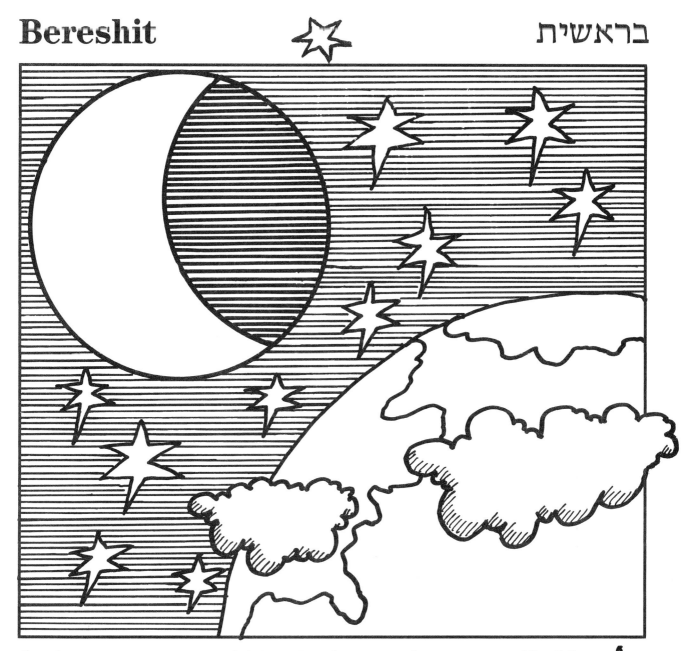

God creates the world in six days and rests on Shabbat. **Everything God creates is very good.**

Adam and Eve are the first two people. They live in the Garden of Eden. It is a wonderful, beautiful place. But, God asks them to leave the Garden after they eat from the **Tree of Knowledge of Good and Evil.**

Abel and Cain are the first children. They fight. Cain kills Abel. When it is too late, Cain learns that he should have been his **brother's keeper.**

Bereshit

 # Help God finish creation

God created the world, but people have to help make it the best possible place.

Day One
God creates light and darkness. *Fill in the darkness.*

Darkness

Light

A second Day
God divides the waters. *Color in the waters.*

Waters Above

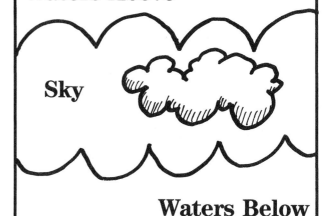

Sky

Waters Below

A third Day
Dry land appears. *Connect the dots to finish this flower.*

A fourth Day
God makes the sun, moon, and stars. *Complete the stars.*

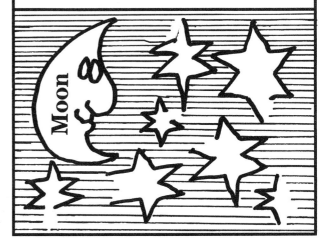

Moon

A fifth Day
God makes fish and birds. *Color the birds and draw more fish.*

The sixth Day
God makes animals and people. *Put the faces on the people.*

The seventh Day
God rests. *Draw the flames on the Shabbat candles.*

Quotation

God said: "Let Us make people in Our image. Let them rule over the fish and birds, over the beasts and the creeping things."

Genesis 1.26

Discuss
What does it mean to be created in God's image?

My Comment
To be like God, I should _____ .

Bereshit

God saw everything God had made. It was very good.

Noah

נח

God sees that living things are **doing evil**. God is unhappy. God picks Noah and his family to build an ark and start over. They are the **one righteous family** in the whole world.

It rains for forty days and forty nights. Everything is **destroyed**. Then the waters go down. God puts a rainbow in the sky and promises, "**Never again** will the earth be destroyed." God says, "**The rainbow is the sign of My promise**."

People get together to build a **tower** so tall that it could reach to God. God thinks that is stupid and **babbles** everyone's language. People spread out and move all over the place.

Find the Right Partner

Noah had to take two of every kind of animal with him on the ark. *Put a circle around the right partner for each animal.*

1. Sheep

2. Lion

3. Dove

4. Hippopotamus

5. Brontosaurus

"In twos, every kind of living thing came to Noah, to the ark."

Noah

The Sign of the Promise

red

yellow

green

blue

violet

God put a rainbow in the
sky as a sign of the promise.
Color the rainbow.

Quotation

God said, "Whenever I cloud the skies
with clouds—
whenever a rainbow appears
in those clouds
I will remember My promise.
NEVER AGAIN will there be a flood
to destroy the earth."

Genesis 9.14-15

Discuss
God promised people that the world would never again be
destroyed. What should we promise God?

My Comment

God promised to never destroy the earth.
One way I could be like God and protect
the earth is by _____.

Lekh-Lekha לֶךְ לְךָ

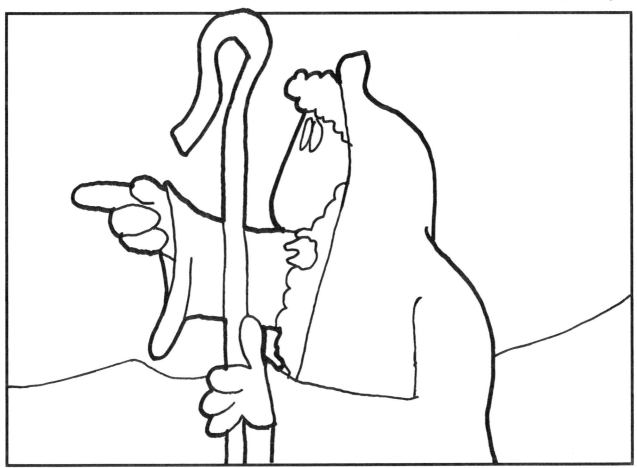

God tells Abram to move his family to the land of Canaan.
God makes two promises. First, God promises to make
Abram's future-family into a **great nation**. Second, God
promises to **give the land of Canaan** to Abram's
future-family. Abram, his wife Sarai and his nephew Lot
move to **Canaan**.

There is not enough food to eat in Canaan. The family
goes to Egypt. Later they return to Canaan. When they
return, there is fighting between the people watching
Abram's herd and the people watching Lot's herd. To keep
the peace, they split up and go their own ways.

God changes Abram's name to **Abraham.** God changes
Sarai's name to **Sarah.**

Count the Stars

God makes two promises to Abram. In the first promise, God tells Abram that his future-family will have as many people as there are stars in the sky. *Count the stars you see in this picture. Color them as you find them.*

How many stars did you find? _____
If you go out at night and count the stars in the sky, how many will you find? _____

The Promised Land

God makes a second promise. God also promises to give a special land to Abram's future-family. Once this land was called Canaan. Today this land is called Israel. It still belongs to the Jewish people. *Color in this map.*

Use these colors.
1—BLUE 2—GREEN 3—BROWN 4—RED 5—YELLOW

Quotation

God said, "And I will make you a great nation.
And I will bless you.
And I will make your name great.
And you will be a blessing."

Genesis 12.2

Discuss
How was Abram special?

 My Comment

God told Abram that he would be a blessing. One way I can be a blessing is by _____ .

Va-yera

Abraham **sees three visitors**. He **runs** to them and **hurries** to make them welcome. He feeds them and gives them a place to rest. The three visitors are messengers from God. They promise that Abraham and Sarah will have a son. Sarah is an old woman. She **laughs**.

God tells Abraham that the cities of **Sodom and Gemorrah will be destroyed**. Abraham makes God promise not to destroy the cities if **ten righteous people** can be found. Lot and his family live in Sodom. They are the only righteous people. They escape and the cities are destroyed.

Abraham and Sarah have **a son named Isaac**. Isaac means "laughter."

Help Abraham Welcome The Visitors

Show Abraham the fastest way to make the visitors welcome. *Draw the path he should follow.*

1. Go to visitors.
2. Go to calf.
3. Go to Sarah.
4. Return to visitors.

Find the Things Needed
to Make the Visitors Feel Welcome

Color in the pictures as you find them.
pitcher of water   bread   calf   plate   fork   knife   spoon

Va-yera

Quotation

The LORD said:
"I have come close to ABRAM
so that he will command his children
and his future-family
to keep the way of the LORD,
to do what is right and just."

Genesis 18.19

Discuss
Why is making someone feel welcome an important mitzvah?

My Comment

One way I can do the *mitzvah* of making someone feel
welcome is by_____.

Ḥaye Sarah חיי שרה

Abraham and Sarah live in Canaan, but they don't own any land. They move from place to place. **Sarah dies**. Abraham **buys a cave** near the city of Hebron. He buries Sarah in that cave.

Abraham wants his son Isaac to marry a girl from his homeland. Abraham **sends his servant** back to the land where he had been born. The servant plans **a test to find the right woman**. Rebekah is picked because she **runs and hurries to make strangers welcome**. She is the right wife for Abraham's son.

The servant brings her home. Rebekah and Isaac fall in love. Later, Abraham dies.

Finding the Right Wife

Finding the right person to marry can be very hard. The servant found Rebekah with a test. *Number the pictures to tell the story of Rebekah's test.*

☐ Rebekah **hurries** to give the man water.

☐ Abraham's servant goes to Abraham's homeland.

☐ Rebekah runs to get more water for all the camels.

☐ Rebekah comes with a jar of water.

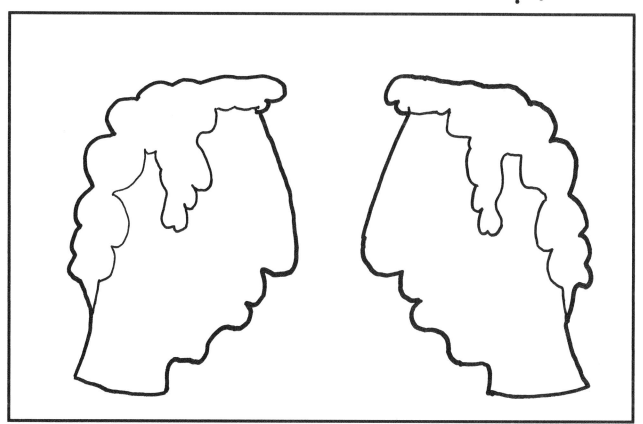

Draw Isaac's face when he learns that Sarah is dead.
Draw Isaac's face when he meets Rebekah.

Quotation

Isaac took Rebekah
into his mother Sarah's tent.
He took Rebekah to be his wife.
He loved her.
Isaac found comfort.
after his mother died.

Geneisis 24. 67

Discuss
Why did Rebekah pass the test? How can we be like Rebekah?

My Comment

Isaac loved Rebekah. Rebekah loved Isaac. I am loveable
when I _____ .

Toldot

Rebekah and Isaac want children. Isaac prays to God. Rebekah becomes pregnant with twins. **The two children fight** in her womb. Esau is born first. Jacob is born holding onto Esau's leg. They are born fighting.

Esau and Jacob grow up. One day Esau goes hunting. He is hungry. Very hungry. Jacob is cooking soup. Esau wants the soup. Jacob makes Esau give him his **firstborn right** before giving him any soup.

Esau is Isaac's oldest son. Isaac wants to give Esau a **special blessing**. Jacob is Rebekah's favorite son. She wants him to get Isaac's special blessing. Esau goes out to hunt. Rebekah and Jacob trick Isaac. Jacob pretends to be Esau and gets the special blessing. Esau is angry. Very angry.

Toldot

1. **Hunt**
2. **Hairy**
3. **Jacob**
4. **The Blessing**

Retell this Story

Isaac is old and blind. He is ready to give his special blessing. Help finish the story. *Write the number of the correct answer box on each line.*

A. Isaac wants to give his blessing to _____ .

B. Esau has _____ arms.

C. Rebekah wants the blessing to go to _____ .

D. Jacob has _____ arms.

E. Esau goes out to _____ .

F. Rebekah puts _____ on Jacob's arms.

G. Isaac feels _____ .

H. Isaac gives Jacob _____ .

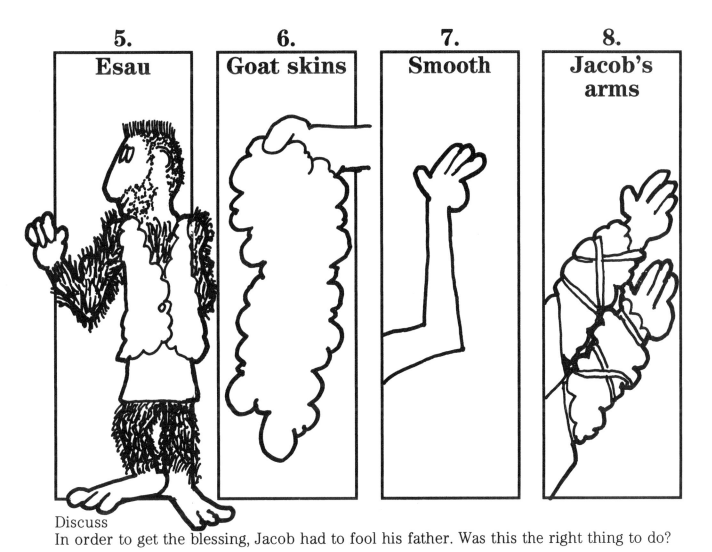

5. Esau — **6. Goat skins** — **7. Smooth** — **8. Jacob's arms**

Discuss
In order to get the blessing, Jacob had to fool his father. Was this the right thing to do?

Quotation

Isaac kissed him and blessed him:
"May God give you from the dew of the sky
and the richness of the earth
and much grain and new wine.
Let those who bless you be blessed."

Genesis 27.27-29

My Comment

The special blessing was Jacob's family treasure. One of my family treasures is _____ .

Va-yetze

וַיֵּצֵא

Jacob runs away. At night, he goes to sleep. He uses a rock as a pillow. He has a **dream**. In that dream, he sees **angels going up and down** the ladder. In that dream, God promises to protect him.

Jacob leaves Canaan and goes to his mother Rebekah's family. He meets a women named Rachel. They fall in love. Rachel has an older sister named Leah. Jacob **wants to marry Rachel**. He talks to her father Laban. They make a deal. Jacob has to **work** for Laban **for seven years**.

After seven years, Jacob is ready to marry Rachel. **Laban tricks him**. The bride at the wedding is **Leah**, not Rachel. Jacob has to **work another seven years** to marry Rachel. Jacob's family grows. He has two wives and twelve children. He owns many sheep and cattle. He leaves Laban and returns to Canaan.

Finish This Dream

Connect the dots.

Jacob dreamed that there were angels going up and down on the _____ .

27

Sisters

Jacob worked seven years and married Leah. Then he worked seven more years and married Rachel.

Find LEAH's name seven times. Circle LEAH's name in **red**.

Find RACHEL's name seven times. Circle RACHEL's name in **blue**.

Rachel   Leah

```
X X X X X X X X X X X X X
L E A H X X R X R A C H E L
E X X X L E A H A X X X X E
A X X X X C X C X X X X A
H X X L E A H X H X X X X H
X X R X X X E X E X R X X X
X R A C H E L X L E A H X X
X X C X X X X X X C X X X
X X H X X X X X X H X X X
X L E A H X X X X E X X X
X X L X X R A C H E L X X X
X X X X X X X X X X X X X
```

Jacob said: "For sure, God is in this place and I didn't know it?"

Discuss
Where are the places where you can find God?

Quotation

Jacob dreamed.
Here—a ladder was set up on earth.
Its top reached the sky.
Here—God's angels were going up and down on it.

Genesis 28.12

My Comment

Something I hope for in my dreams is _____

_____

Va-yishlah

After many years, Jacob **returns home**. He gets ready to meet his brother Esau. He is afraid that Esau will still be angry at him. He splits his camp into two in order to protect his family.

In the middle of the night, Jacob meets a stranger. They **wrestle until morning**. The stranger wants to leave. Jacob won't let him go. The stranger hurts Jacob's leg. Jacob still won't let go. Jacob makes the stranger give him a **blessing**. The stranger may be an angel. The blessing is a new name, "Israel." **Jacob becomes Israel**.

Jacob and Esau meet. There is no fighting. They hug and then go in different directions. Rachel dies while giving birth to a son, Benjamin.

Jacob's New Name

A person's name is very important. Sometimes it can tell us what a person is like. In the Torah, when a name is changed, it means that the person has changed too.

Finish these two names:

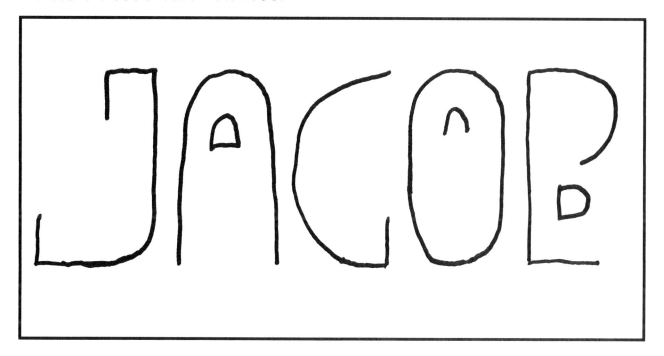

Va-yishlaḥ

By the time Jacob returns to Canaan, his family is complete. *See if you can find all 13 of Jacob's children in the picture. Color them as you find them.*

How many children did you find? _____

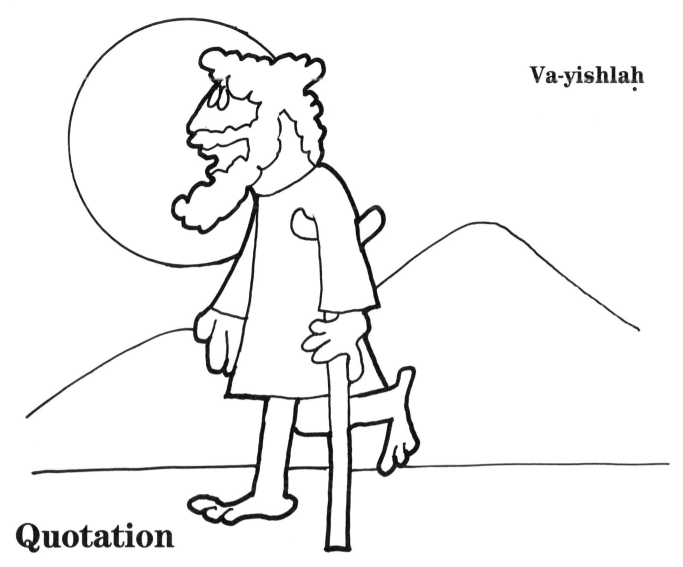

Quotation

He said: "What is your name?"
He said: "Jacob (meaning the one who grabs heels)".
He said: "Jacob is not your name anymore.
Israel (meaning the one who wrestles with God)
is your name,
because you have struggled with God
and with people."

Genesis 32.28-29

Discuss
What does your name teach you?

My Comment

When Jacob's name was changed to Israel, he felt
like a new person. One time I felt like a "new me" was
when_____ .

Va-yeshev

Israel has **twelve sons**. **Joseph is his favorite son**. He gives Joseph a special coat, a **coat of many colors**. Joseph's brothers hate him. Joseph has **two dreams**. In one dream, all of his brothers' bundles of grain bow down to his bundle of grain. In the other dream, the sun, the moon, and eleven stars all bow down to him. After Joseph tells about the dreams, the brothers hate him more.

Once, Israel sends Joseph to find his brothers. They are watching the sheep. When he finds them, they **throw him in a pit**. Later, they sell him to some merchants. The merchants bring him to Egypt and sell him as a slave. At first, everything is good. Joseph is **his master's favorite**. Then he gets in trouble and is **thrown in jail**.

In jail, Joseph again becomes **the favorite**. He meets the King's butler and baker. They each have a dream. Joseph **explains their dreams**.

34

Retell this Story

The story of Joseph is a very important story. *Circle the right word needed to finish each sentence.*

Joseph gets a _____
coat   teddy-bear

Joseph has 2 _____
cats   dreams

Joseph's brothers throw him in a
_____.
telephone booth pit

Joseph is sold and taken to _____.
Egypt   New York

Joseph becomes a
_____.
ballet dancer slave

Joseph is thrown in
_____.
jail   a bath tub

Joseph explains the meaning of 2 _____
dreams   penguins

The Coat of Many Colors

Make Joseph's coat full of many colors. How many different colors did you use? _____

Quotation

Even in the dungeon, the LORD was with Joseph.
Joseph found favor in the eyes of the dungeon-master
Everything he did, the LORD made succeed.

Genesis 39.21-23

Discuss
God was with Joseph when he was in slavery in Egypt. God was with Joseph when he was in jail. How can God be everywhere?

My Comment

Wherever Joseph was, God was with him. One time I felt that God was with me was when _____

_____

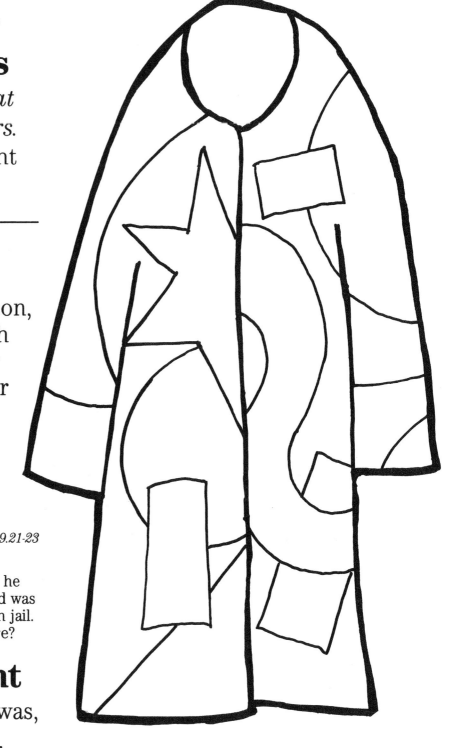

Miketz

מקץ

Pharaoh has **two dreams**. In one dream, seven thin cows eat seven fat cows. In the other dream, seven thin ears of grain eat seven fat ears of grain. No one knows what these dreams mean. The King's butler remembers Joseph. He remembers that Joseph explained his dream. The King sends for Joseph. Joseph explains that the dreams mean there will be **seven good fat years which will be followed by seven years of famine.**

Joseph becomes the **King's favorite**. Joseph is in charge of all Egypt. For seven years, they save up all the extra food. When the seven years of famine come, there is enough food for everyone.

The famine comes to Canaan. Israel sends ten of his sons to Egypt to buy grain. **They come to Joseph**. Joseph tricks his brothers and pretends to be an Egyptian. He **tests** them. He says that when they come for more food, they must bring Benjamin, the youngest son. When they return, Joseph tricks them by hiding gold in Benjamin's bag. Benjamin looks like a thief.

Miketz

Read this Story

Here is a story with words and pictures. See if you can read it!

Phar + [boat] was the [crown] of Egypt.

1 night Phar + [boat] had a dream.

He did [knot] **No** what the dream meant.

Phar + [boat] . [1¢] for Joseph. [coat]

[coat] was in [jail] .

[coat] told Phar + [boat] :

" **U U U** [saw] 7 fat [cow]'s

[saw] 7 fat [ear]'s of g + [grain]

will have 7 [happy face] y + [ear]'s .

Then **U** [saw] 7 thin [cow]'s .

U [saw] 7 thin [ear]'s of g+ [grain]

U will have 7 [sad face] y + [ear]'s .

God is telling you to plan a [cloud] . "

Now it is your turn to draw:

fat cow	thin cow	fat ear of grain	thin ear of grain
	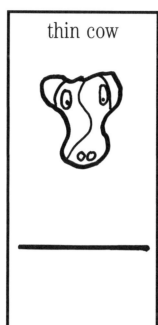	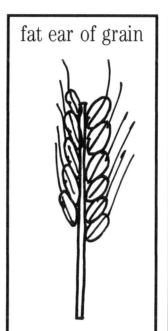	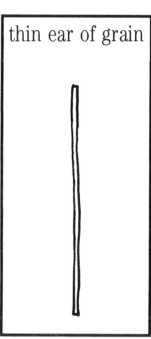

Quotation

The famine was everywhere.
Joseph opened all the storehouses
and gave shares of grain to the
Egyptians.
There was great hunger in Egypt.
From all the earth, people came to Egypt
to get food from Joseph.

Genesis 42.56

Discuss
Why did Joseph give away Egyptian food to people who
weren't from Egypt?

My Comment

Joseph helped his family. He also
helped all the people who were hungry.
One way I could be like Joseph and
help people is by _____

Va-yigash

ויגש

The brothers believe that Benjamin will become a slave in Egypt. They are **afraid** to tell their father, Israel, that another son has been lost. **Judah begs Joseph** to let Benjamin go. He offers to stay in Benjamin's place. Joseph cries.

Joseph stops pretending. He tells Israel's sons that he is their long-lost brother Joseph. They hug and cry. He tells them, **"God sent me ahead of you to save lives."**

Pharaoh welcomes Joseph's family. Israel **brings the whole family to Egypt**. They settle in an area called Goshen.

Put it Back Together

In this story the puzzle of "Who is Joseph?" is solved. Can you solve these puzzles? *Match the top and bottom of each picture by drawing a line.*

Pharaoh   Joseph   Benjamin   Israel

Va-yigash

Whose Name is Hidden?

Color in all of the spaces with a dot. What name do you see?

Quotation

Joseph said: "Please, come close to me."
They came close, and he said: "I am Joseph your brother, the one you sold into Egypt.
Now, do not be pained. Do not feel guilty that you sold me. God sent me before you to save life."

Genesis 45.4-5

Discuss
How can you be very angry at a brother or a sister and still love him or her very much?

My Comment

Joseph was able to teach his brothers an important lesson. One time when I taught something important to others was when I _____

Va-yeḥi

Israel is very old. Joseph brings his two sons **Ephraim and Manasseh** to see his father. Israel **blesses** Joseph's sons. Then Israel blesses each of his own twelve sons. Before he dies, Israel makes his sons promise to bury him in the **land of Canaan.**

Israel dies. His sons bring his body back to the land which God promised to give to Abraham's future-family. After Israel dies, Joseph again tells his brothers that he has forgiven them for all they did to him when he was a boy. He tells them, "Someday, **God will bring you back to the Promised Land.**" He makes them promise to carry his bones back with them. Then Joseph, too, dies.

43

Va-yeḥi

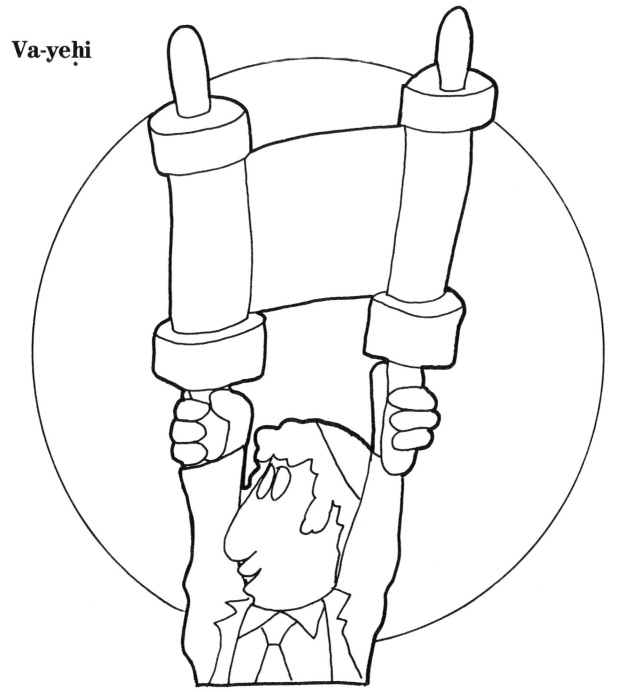

When we finish reading a book of the Torah, we say, "*Ḥazak, Ḥazak, v'nithazeik.*" It means, "Be strong, very strong, and let us grow stronger together." We are very proud of what we have learned and we look forward to learning even more.

My Comment

One story I really liked in the book of Bereshit was _____ .

Abraham's Family

ABRAHAM

SARAH

ISAAC

REBEKAH

RACHEL

JACOB

LEAH

JOSEPH

This is the last sidrah in the book of Bereshit. You have learned the stories of many people in our Jewish family. *Cut out the pictures and paste them in the right places on our Jewish family tree.*

SARAH

ISAAC

LEAH

JACOB

JOSEPH

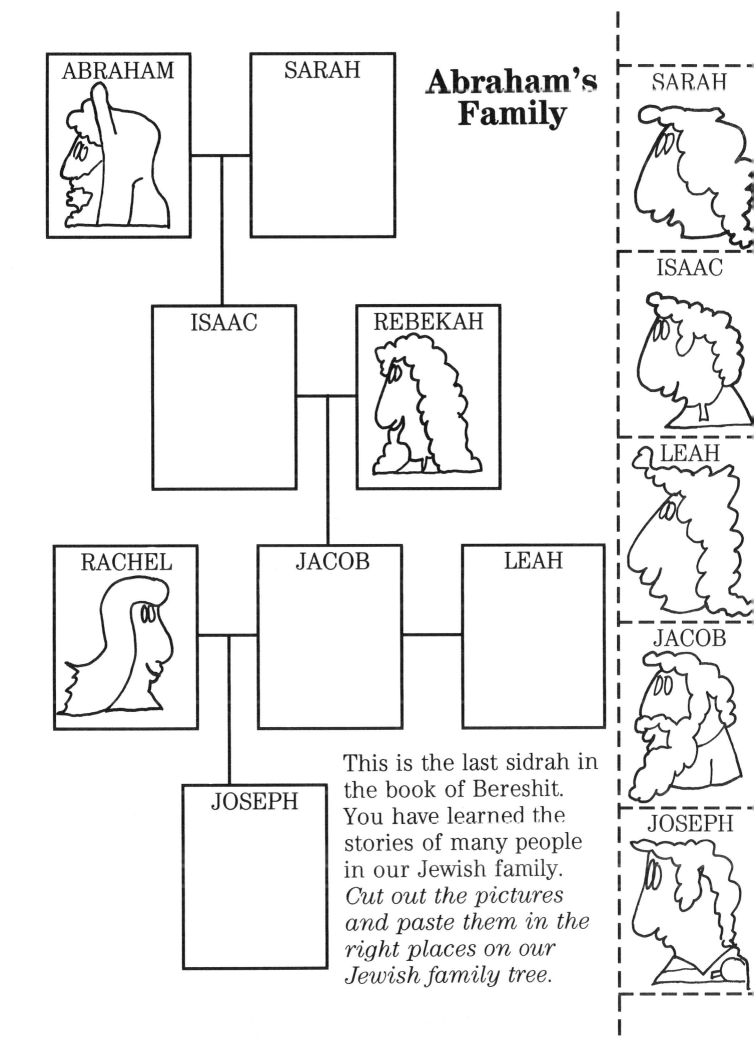

Shcmot

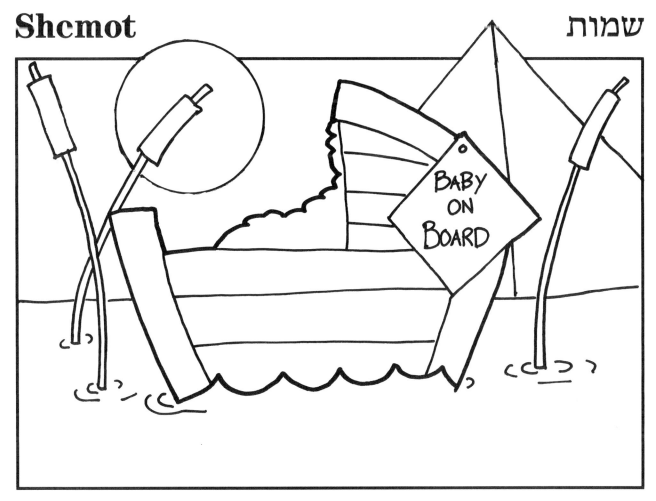

When Israel came to Egypt, there were only **seventy people** in the whole family. Now, the family has grown to six hundred thousand people. Egypt has **a new Pharaoh who doesn't remember Joseph**. He is afraid of the Jewish people. **He turns them into slaves** and makes them work hard. He **makes their lives bitter**. He orders his people to kill all newborn Jewish boys.

A Jewish woman has a son. She **hides her son in a basket** which she floats on the Nile River. Pharaoh's daughter finds the baby. She names him **Moses** and raises him as her own son. When he grows up, he sees an Egyptian hitting a Jew. To stop the beating, **Moses kills the Egyptian**. He runs away to a country called Midian. At the well there, he meets a woman who becomes his wife.

Shemot

Moses becomes a shepherd. One day he sees a **burning bush** which doesn't burn up. God speaks to him from that bush. God tells Moses to **go back to Egypt and lead Israel's children to freedom** in the Promised Land.

Put an X next to the sentence that goes with the picture.

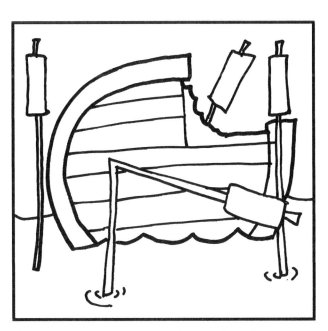

☐ Here is Moses in a basket.
☐ Here is Moses in a bottle.

☐ Moses is found by Pharaoh's son.
☐ Moses is found by Pharaoh's daughter.

☐ Moses meets his wife by the well.
☐ Moses meets his wife by the mall.

☐ Moses saw a bush that did not burn up.
☐ Moses saw a bush that blasted off.

Help Moses Find the Burning Bush

Quotation

When Moses grew up
he went out to his brothers.
He saw their suffering.

Exodus 2.11

Discuss
Moses lived in Pharaoh's palace. He did not need to see or know about the suffering of slaves. Caring about other people made him a good Jew. Where is there suffering that we should see?

My Comment

It made Moses very angry when he saw one person hurting another. It makes me angry when I see _____ .

Moses and his brother Aaron go to Pharaoh. They tell him, "God said, '**Let My People Go**.'" Aaron throws his staff down on the ground. It turns into a snake. The men who do magic for Pharaoh throw their staffs onto the ground, too. Their staffs also turn into snakes. Aaron's staff eats all of their staffs.

When Pharaoh says "No," God turns the Nile river into **blood**. All the water in Egypt turns into blood. This is the first plague. Next, God fills Egypt with **frogs**. Frogs are everywhere. This is the second plague. Then God puts **lice** all over Egypt. Every living thing in Egypt has lice. Lice are the third plague. Next God fills all of Egypt with **bugs**. Insects are the fourth plague. During the fifth plague all the **cattle get sick**. For the sixth plague God gives everyone in Egypt **itchy skin**. The seventh plague is big **hail** which falls like rain. Still, Pharaoh won't let the Jewish people go.

Frogs

The second plague God sent to Egypt was frogs. There were frogs all over the place. There are frogs all over these pages, too. *Color all the frogs you can find in this picture.*

How many did you find _____?
The word FROG is hidden ten times on this page. *Circle all ten.*

Draw the missing half of this frog. Then color the whole frog.

Color the first frog green. Make blue spots on the second frog. Color the third frog red and purple.

Quotation

And the LORD spoke to Moses.
"Go to Pharaoh and say to him:
'Let my people go.
And if you refuse to let them go,
I will fill your land with frogs.
They will come into your house,
and into your bed,
and into your ovens,
and into your bread pans'."
And the frogs came up
and covered the land of Egypt.

Exodus 7.26-28

Discuss
Read the first seven plagues again. Which do you think would be the worst?

My Comment

Moses told Pharaoh, "Let my people go." One time I wished someone would let me go was when_____

God has already sent seven plagues to Egypt. Still, Pharaoh won't let the Jewish people go. Next God sends **locust bugs** which eat up all the food growing in Egypt. Locusts are the eighth plague. Still, Pharaoh doesn't change his mind. God makes all of Egypt **dark** as midnight. Darkness is the ninth plague. Still the Jewish people are slaves. The tenth plague is the last plague. On this night **every firstborn Egyptian child dies**, but God passes over all the Jewish homes. All of the Jewish children are safe.

On the last night in Egypt, God has Moses and Aaron tell every Jewish family to celebrate Passover. Each family celebrates with a **Passover lamb**, some **bitter herbs**, and **matzah**. In the morning, Pharaoh finally changes his mind. The Jewish people leave Egypt.

Seder Things

Every year at Passover we remember this sidrah. We eat special foods and put a special plate on our table. We remember when we were slaves in Egypt and how God led us to freedom.

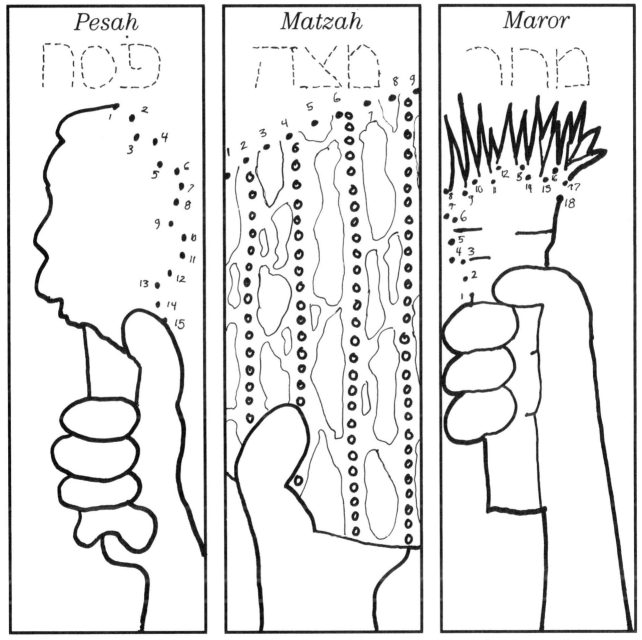

Pesah *Matzah* *Maror*

Connect the dots to see the three symbols of the seder. Trace the names of these symbols.

Bo

To keep the Jewish people safe, God told them to paint the doorpost of their houses. *Find the dot on each doorpost and put a red letter* **shin** *there.*

Today, Jews put a mezuzah on their doorposts. It makes them feel safe.

Help make this mezuzah beautiful.
Color the Hebrew letter **shin** (ש) *blue.*
Color the Hebrew letter **dalet** (ד) *green.*
Color the Hebrew letter **yud** (י) *red.*

Quotation

You shall eat Matzah for seven days.
And you should tell your children on that day:
This is done because of what the Lord did for me
when I came out of Egypt.

Exodus 13.8

Discuss
Every year when we celebrate Passover, we remember that once we were slaves. Why is it important to remember that we were once slaves?

My Comment

Passover reminds us of the time God took us out of Egypt. The symbol of Passover that means the most to me is _____.

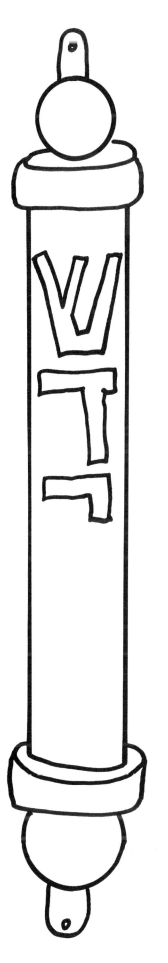

57

Beshallaḥ

בשלח

Israel's family is leaving Egypt. God leads them to the **Sea of Reeds**. Then, Pharaoh changes his mind again. He wants the Jewish people back. He takes his soldiers and chases them. Pharaoh catches them at the Reed Sea. **God divides the Sea**. The Jewish people cross by walking on dry land. When the Egyptian army follows them, the waters return and the Egyptian soldiers drown.

When they are safe, the Jewish people sing thank you songs to God. Later, the people complain about water. They are afraid that they will find no water in the wilderness. Moses finds them sweet water. Every day God feeds them with **a special food called manna**. Once again, the people complain about water. This time **God tells Moses to touch a rock** with his staff. Moses hits the rock and water pours out. An evil people named Amalek attack Israel, but the Jewish people win.

Retell this Story

Number these pictures in the correct order.

The water covers up the Egyptian soldiers.

Moses leads the Jews to the Sea of Reeds.

The Reed Sea splits. The Jews cross over.

The Egyptian soldiers chase after the Jews.

Beshallaḥ

Life in the Wilderness

It was hard to find food and water in the wilderness, but God made sure that the Jews had what they needed.
Cross out the things that do not belong in this picture.

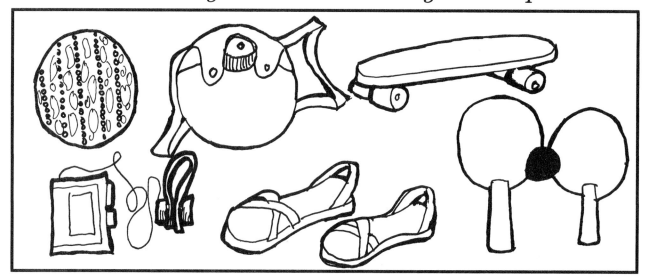

Were there telephones in the time of Moses _____?

Quotation

And Moses put his hand over the sea,
and the LORD made the sea go back,
and made the sea dry land,
and the waters were divided.
And the Children of Israel
went into the middle of the sea
on dry land.

Exodus 14.21-22

Discuss
What would it be like to spend 40 years in the Sinai wilderness?

My Comment

When the Jews were able to walk across the Reed Sea it was a miracle. Something that I think is a miracle is _____ .

The Family of Israel hiked from Ra'amses to Sukkot almost 600,000 people.
They baked the dough which they brought out of Egypt into Matzah because it did not have time to rise.

Exodus 12.37-39

Yitro

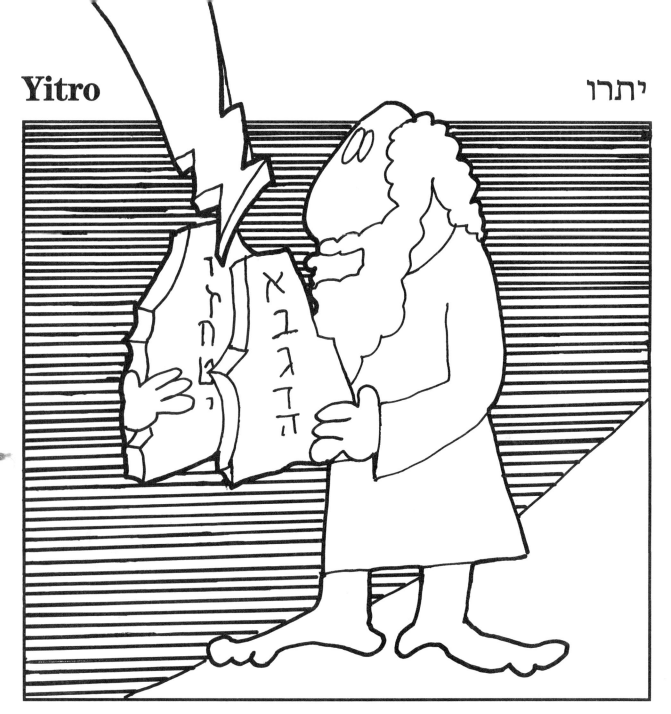

Jethro is the father of Moses' wife. Jethro hears the news about all that God has done for Moses and his people Israel. He brings Moses' wife and son to join him. Jethro teaches Moses that he **needs help judging and leading the people.**

Moses leads the people to **Mount Sinai**, the same place where he saw the burning bush. God orders them to get ready. There is thunder. Mount Sinai smokes. God teaches the people the **Ten Commandments.**

1. I am the Lord your God.
2. No idols or other gods.
3. No saying "I swear to God" when telling a lie.
4. Remember the Shabbat.
5. Honor your father and mother.
6. No murder.
7. Be faithful to your husband or wife.
8. No stealing.
9. No lying when you are a witness.
10. No wishing to take things which belong to someone else.

All of the people say, "All that the Lord has taught—we will do."

Yitro

Moses wrote the words of the Ten Commandments on two tablets of stone. *Finish this picture of the tablets.*

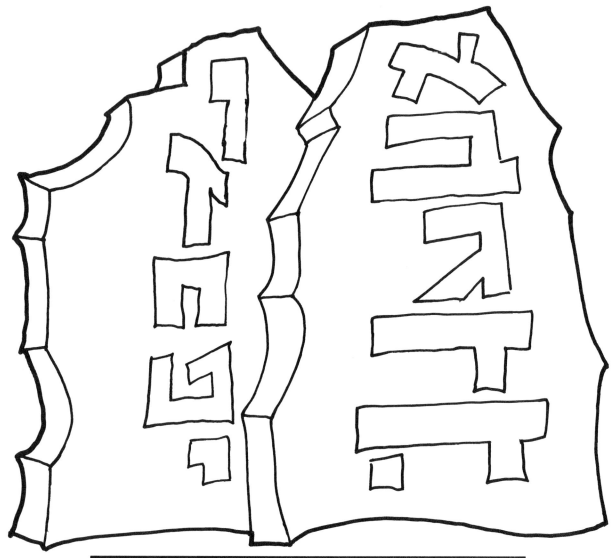

Color the Hebrew letter **Alef** א	*blue.*
Color the Hebrew letter **Bet** ב	*green.*
Color the Hebrew letter **Gimel** ג	*yellow.*
Color the Hebrew letter **Dalet** ד	*orange.*
Color the Hebrew letter **Hey** ה	*red.*
Color the Hebrew letter **Vav** ו	*brown.*
Color the Hebrew letter **Zayin** ז	*black.*
Color the Hebrew letter **Het** ח	*purple.*
Color the Hebrew letter **Tet** ט	*pink.*
Color the Hebrew letter **Yud** י	*grey.*

The fourth commandment tells us to remember the Shabbat. *Circle all of the things which remind you of Shabbat.*

Quotation

If you will listen to My voice,
and keep My covenant,
then you will be
My own treasure
from among the peoples.

Exodus 19.5

Discuss:
What is one of your favorite Shabbat things?

My Comment

The fifth commandment tells us to honor our parents. One way I can do the mitzvah of honoring my parents is by _____ .

Mishpatim

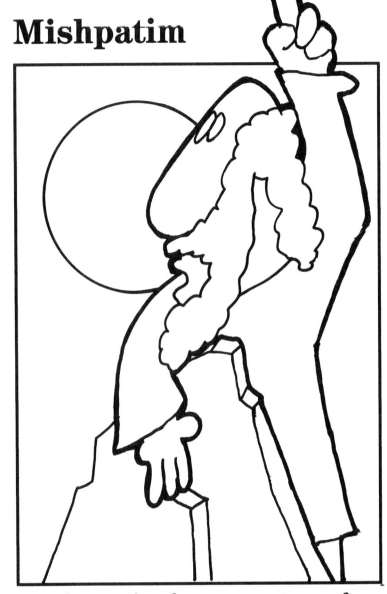

Next, God teaches the Jewish people a lot of laws. These laws help people to live together in peace and justice. There are laws about slaves and when they should be set free. There are laws about fighting, about murder, and about when you hurt someone by accident.

There are many laws about being responsible. We are taught that if you own an ox who hurts another animal, you must pay for what is injured. We are taught that if you dig a pit and something falls into it, you must pay for what is broken. We are taught that if your sheep eat someone else's crops, you must pay for the crops. We are also taught that if you start a fire and it spreads by accident, you must pay for what is burned.

God teaches the Jewish people many more laws. Moses reads the whole Book of the Covenant to the people and they say, "**We will do and we will listen.**" Then Moses goes up **Mount Sinai** to spend **40 days and 40 nights** writing down the commandments.

Judge these Cases

The laws in this sidrah were not just for people long ago. We should follow them today. *Put an X next to the right thing to do.*

If your ox hurts another animal:

☐ Pay for the damage.
☐ Do nothing.

If you dig a pit and something falls in:

☐ Pay for the damage.
☐ Do nothing.

If your sheep eat someone else's crops:

☐ Pay for the damage.
☐ Do nothing.

If you start a fire and it spreads:

☐ Pay for the damage.
☐ Do nothing.

Mishpatim

If your cat hurts another animal:

☐ Pay for the damage.
☐ Do nothing.

If you leave your roller skates out and someone trips on them:

☐ Pay for the damage.
☐ Do nothing.

If your dog eats something it shouldn't:

☐ Pay for the damage.
☐ Do nothing.

Quotation

And Moses told the people all the words of the LORD and all the judgments, and all the people answered with one voice and said: "All the things which the Lord said we will do."

Exodus 24.3

Discuss

All these laws teach us that if we cause damage, we must be responsible and pay for that damage. They also remind us to be careful. How could we keep the damage from happening in each of these cases?

My Comment

All of the laws in this sidrah teach us to be responsible.
One way I must be responsible is _____ .

Terumah תרומה

God gives Moses the plans to build the **Mishkan**. The Mishkan is a place where the Jewish people can worship God. The Mishkan can be folded up and moved from place to place. It is a worship place that the Jewish people can use in the wilderness.

Moses asks the Jewish people to donate gifts. He asks them to give **gold, silver, copper, cloth, furs**, and **jewels**. All of these gifts will be used to build the Mishkan.

The Mishkan will be a big tent. Big boards will make up the sides. The top will be covered with cloth and skins. Inside the Mishkan there will be the **ark**, the **table**, and the **menorah**.

Terumah

Connect the dots to make the tent of the Mishkan.

Inside the Mishkan are the ark, the table, and the menorah. *Finish the ark.*

Put a loaf of bread on every shelf.
How many loaves of bread did you make? _____

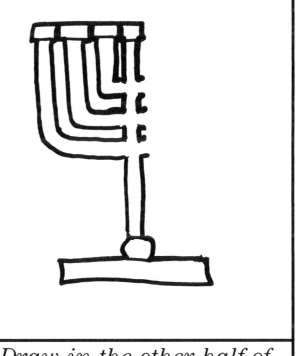

Draw in the other half of the menorah. Add flames to each branch of the menorah.
How many flames did you light? _____

Terumah

Quotation

And the LORD spoke to Moses and said:
Tell the children of Israel
to bring me a gift;
you shall take a gift from
every person whose
heart tells him to give.

Exodus 25.1

Discuss
The Mishkan was the special worship place Israel's family built in the wilderness. What is your family's worship place? What is it like to go to synagogue?

My Comment

In this sidrah many people bring gifts to God. One way I could give God a gift is by _____ .

Tetzaveh

תצוה

Aaron and Moses are brothers. They come from the Kohen family of the tribe of Levi. God picks Aaron and his sons to be the **Kohanim**, those leading the worship services in the Mishkan.

God gives directions to make special clothes for Aaron who will be the first **Head Kohein**. Aaron is to wear a **special robe with fringes**, an **apron**, a **breastplate** with 12 stones, and a **special hat** with a **gold headband**. God even gives directions for making for Aaron's underwear.

Next, God tells how to have a special worship service so that Aaron and his sons can begin their turn as Kohanim. The Kohanim will take care of the Mishkan. The Mishkan is the special place where Israel's family can go to be close to God.

Tetzaveh

The Breastplate

The breastplate which the Head Kohein wore was very fancy. There were four rows of stones. Each stone was for one of the tribes in Israel's family. *Color each stone.*

How many stones did you color? _____

Quotation

Take Aaron, your brother, and his sons with him from among the Children of Israel that he may serve me in the special job of priest.

Exodus 28.1

Discuss
In ancient days, being a Kohein was a major Jewish job. What are some of today's Jewish jobs?

My Comment

Aaron and his sons were given the special job of being Kohanim. One special job I have is _____ .

Help Dress Aaron

The Kohanim got to dress in many fancy clothes. *Color in the clothes that the Kohanim wore. Cut them out.*

1. *Put on the special robe with fringes.*
2. *Put on the apron.*
3. *Put the breastplate on top.*
4. *Put on the hat.*

75

Tetzaveh

Ki Tissa

כי תשא

God tells Moses how to count how many people are now in Israel's family. God also gives the plans for making a **washing stand**, a **special oil**, and the **incense** which will be used in the Mishkan.

A man named **Bezalel** is made the head artist. Bezalel will be in charge of all the work of building the Mishkan. In the middle of telling about all the things which will have to be built, God reminds the Jewish people that **no work can be done on Shabbat**.

Ki Tissa

Moses has been gone a long time up on Mt. Sinai. The people are afraid that he will not come back. They give up. They build an idol, **a golden calf**. When Moses comes down the mountain carrying the two stone tablets with the Ten Commandments written on them, he sees the people worshiping this idol. He gets very angry. He **smashes the tablets** of the Ten Commandments. He burns the golden calf. He forces the Jewish people to make up for what they have done wrong.

God orders Moses to go back up Mt. Sinai and carve the Ten Commandments on **new tablets**.

Retell this Story

Circle YES or NO for each sentence.

Moses was up on Mt. Sinai for a long time.
YES NO

The people were afraid he would not come back.
YES NO

The people built a silver cow.
YES NO

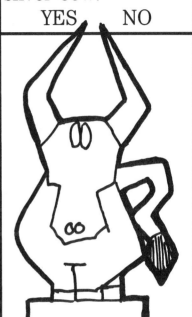

The people prayed to the Golden Calf.
YES NO

When Moses came down and saw what the people were doing, he was happy.
YES NO

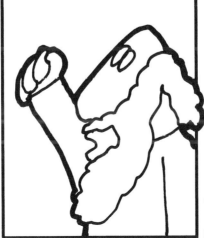

Moses was so angry that he broke the tablets of the Ten Commandments.
YES NO

Ki Tissa

The tablets of the Ten Commandments broke into many pieces when Moses threw them down. *Find all the broken pieces.* HINT: Each piece has a Hebrew letter on it.

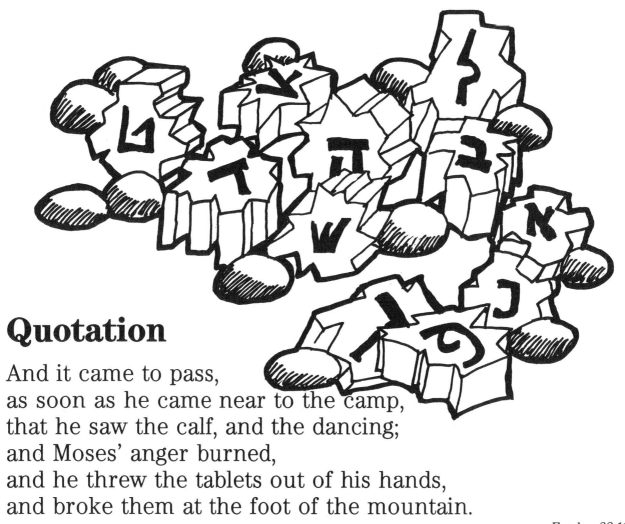

Quotation

And it came to pass,
as soon as he came near to the camp,
that he saw the calf, and the dancing;
and Moses' anger burned,
and he threw the tablets out of his hands,
and broke them at the foot of the mountain.

Exodus 32.19

Discuss:
The people knew that worshiping an idol was wrong. Still when Moses was gone a long time, they built the Golden Calf. Why did they do something they know was wrong?

My Comment

Moses got very angry with the Jewish people because making the Golden Calf broke one of the Ten Commandments.

Once I made someone very angry by _____ .

Va-yak-hel

Moses gathers all the Jewish people together. Again he reminds them that no work can be done on Shabbat. Then he goes over all the plans for the Mishkan.

Bezalel leads the Jewish people in doing the work. All the gold, silver, copper, animal skins, cloth, and jewels which the people have given as gifts are used. They make the **Mishkan** and the **cloths** which cover it. They make the **ark**, the **table**, and the **menorah**. They make the **washing stand** and the **incense altar**. They make the **big altar** with horns where Aaron will make the offerings. They make everything.

Believe it or not, the Jewish people bring **too many gifts**. Moses has to tell them that they have given enough.

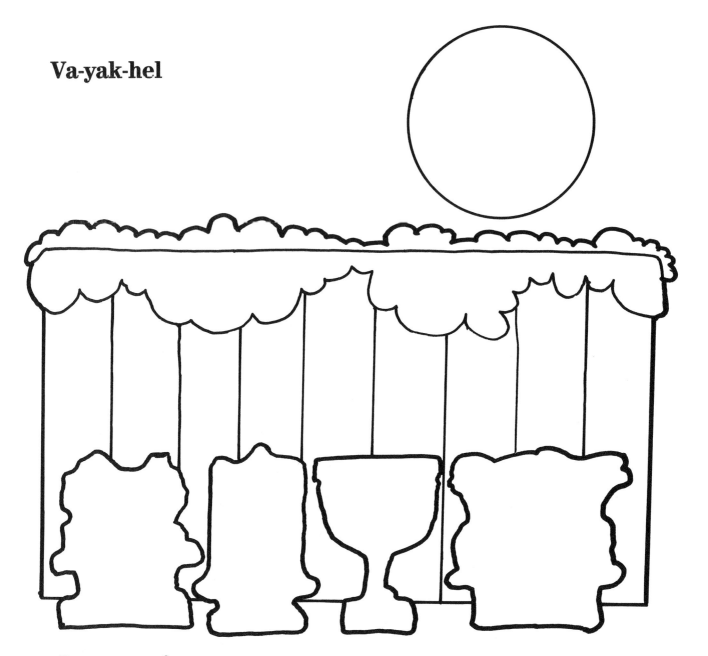

Quotation

See, the LORD has picked Bezalel
and he has filled him with the spirit of God
with wisdom and many skills
and told him to make
many beautiful works of art.

Exodus 35.30-33

My Comment

Bezalel had a special skill for making beautiful things. A special skill I have is _____ .

It is time to get the Mishkan ready.
1. *Color each object.*
2. *Cut it out.*
3. *Paste it in the right place.*
4. *Color in the rest of the picture.*

Ark

Table

Menorah

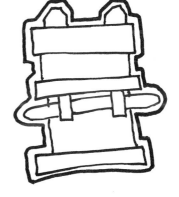

Altar for offerings

Va-yak-hel

Pekudei פקודי

All the work on the Mishkan, the things which go in it, and the special clothing for the Head Kohein are **finished**. Moses gives a report of all the gifts which were given and how they were used.

The Mishkan is set up for the first time. Aaron puts on his Head Kohein clothes for the first time. There is a special service to mark this first time. Moses puts the tablets in the ark. He puts bread on the table and he lights the menorah. Then, Moses hangs the curtain on the front of the Mishkan.

When the Mishkan is finished, God can be found there. During the day, there is a **cloud over the Mishkan**. During the night, there is a **column of fire**.

Pekudei

This is the last sidrah in the Book of Shemot. Israel's family has come a long way. Play this game with someone else. It will help you remember all the things that have happened to Israel's family.

Joseph moves the whole family to Egypt.

Go ahead one square for every person from our Jewish family tree you can name.

There is a new Pharaoh who does not know Joseph *Lose one turn.*

Moses is born and hidden.

Moses leaves Egypt.

Moses sees two men fighting.

Go ahead one square if you remember who found Moses.

Moses sees the burning bush.

Go ahead two squares if you can remember what was special about the burning bush.

Moses and Aaron visit Pharaoh. The ten plagues begin.

Go ahead one square for each plague you ca[n] name.

Mt. Sinai.

Go ahead one square for each of the Ten Commandments you can say.

Hazak, Hazak, V'nithazeik.

Go ahead one square if you can tell what came out of the rock.

Lose one turn making the Golden Calf.

Moses hits the rock.

Moses gets a new set of tablets.

You have finished reading the Book of Shemot.

Manna falls from the sky.

Aaron is made High Priest.

The Mishkan is finished and a special service is held.

Cross the Reed Sea and take another turn.

Bezalel helps to build the Mishkan.

Lose one turn baking Matzah.

Va-yikra

God teaches about the worship services in the Mishkan. In the Mishkan people are to give **gift-offerings** to God. These offerings are sacrifices. A sacrifice is like a barbecue, because food is cooked on the altar.

The **regular offering** is to be made every day. It can be a cooked cow, sheep or goat. It can also be a cooked bird. The **afternoon offering** is to be made of flour and oil. It can be cooked in a pan or made like a pizza. Another kind of offering is for expressing a **hope for peace**. Other kinds of offerings are ways of saying, "**I am sorry** that I did something wrong."

Help Aaron's sons
pick the best animals

Long ago the Jewish people gave gift-offerings to God.
Often these gifts were animals.

1. *Color* 4 birds blue.

2. *Color* 3 sheep black.

3. *Color* 2 goats brown.

4. *Color* 1 cow purple.

Va-yikra

Bible Times and Today

Today, we do not give sacrifices. We do not have a Mishkan with a Head Kohein. *Draw a line and match what Jews did long ago with what we do today.*

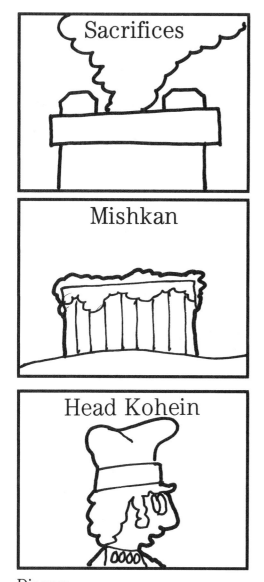

Discuss

In ancient times, a gift-offering was a way of thanking God. What are some ways we can thank God?

My Comment

In this part of the Torah, God teaches Moses many rules.

One important rule I will always remember is _____ .

God teaches that there is to be **an always-burning flame** on the altar. Aaron and his sons always have to be ready to make an offering. There is to be a **morning offering**, an **afternoon offering**, and **an offering made in the evening**. People can also make offerings when they want to say "**thank you**," or when they want to say, "**I am sorry**."

God reviews all the rules for how to make an offering. God teaches everything that the Kohanim are supposed to do. While teaching how to cook the offerings, God orders Jews not to eat any blood, nor to eat meat from an animal which was killed by a wild animal.

Tzav

Morning—Afternoon—Evening

Three times a day Jews thank God for all we have. The first Jews prayed to God in their own way. Israel's family gave thanks in the Mishkan and the Temple. Today, we gather in the synagogue.

Draw the Sun in the right place in each picture.

Morning	Afternoon	Evening	
Abraham gets up early in the morning to pray.	Isaac prays in the afternoon	Jacob prays at night	**The First Jews**
morning offerings	afternoon offerings	evening offerings	**In the Mishkan**
Shaḥarit	**Minḥah**	**Ma'ariv**	**Today**

And the sons of Aaron the Kohein shall put fire upon the altar and pile wood upon the fire.

Leviticus 1.7

Jewish Lights

Here are many different kinds of lights.
Circle the ones which are used in a Jewish way.
*Put an **S** next to the lights used on Shabbat.*
*Put a **H** next to the lights used on Ḥanukkah.*
*And, put a **T** next to the light that never goes out.*

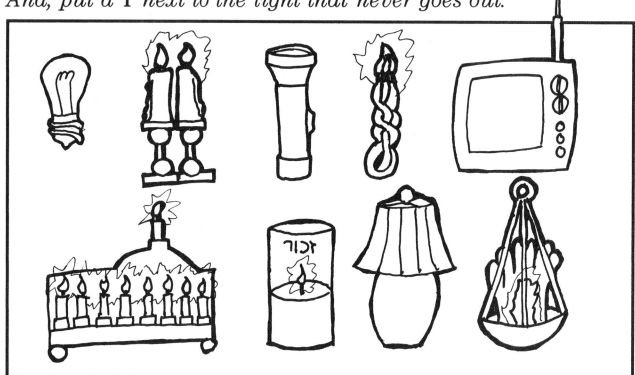

Quotation

Always keep a fire
burning on the altar.
It shall never go out.

Leviticus 6.6

Discuss
What lesson does an always-burning light teach?

My Comment

God ordered the Jewish people to keep an always-burning
light. One thing which I think should last forever
is _____ .

Shemini

שמיני

SCALES →   FINS

The special service to celebrate the start of Aaron's turn as Head Kohein comes to an end. **Moses and Aaron bless the people**. God sends a fire down which burns the offering. The people cheer.

Nadav and **Abihu** are two of Aaron's sons. One night they sneak into the Mishkan. They do something with the incense altar. They are burnt by a strange fire. Later, God has Moses warn Aaron and his sons to be careful about drinking wine or strong drinks before they work in the Mishkan.

Next, God teaches all the rules about what kinds of foods Jews should or should not eat. God teaches that animals which may be eaten must have split **hoofs** and **chew their cud**. Birds which can be eaten must not be hunters. And, edible fish must have both **fins** and **scales**.

Shemini

Split Hoofs

Help Aaron find the right animals. *Color all the animals that have hoofs that are in two or more parts.*

Fins and Scales

Help Miriam find the right fish. *Cross out the seafood which does not have fins and scales.*

Today, many foods that are Kosher have a special sign on the label. All of these signs show that a food is Kosher. *Circle the Kosher signs you find. Color the packages .*

Quotation

You should separate
the holy from the ordinary
and the unclean from the clean—
so you can teach the children of Israel
all the laws that the LORD has spoken.

Exodus 10.10

Discuss
What is Jewish about the way we eat today?

My Comment

One of the jobs of the Kohanim was to teach the people the right thing to do. Someone who teaches me the right thing to do is _____ .

Tazria

תזריע

Aaron and his sons work in the Mishkan and help with the offerings. God also teaches that they are the ones who should help the Jewish people with their health problems, just like today's doctors.

God teaches them what to do for women who have given birth to children, and spends a lot of time teaching them how to cure a very bad skin disease called leprosy.

The Kohanim helped many people who were sick. They did not have as many tools to help them as doctors have today. Here is a picture of a Kohein at work. *Cross out the things that do not belong (because they were not yet invented).*

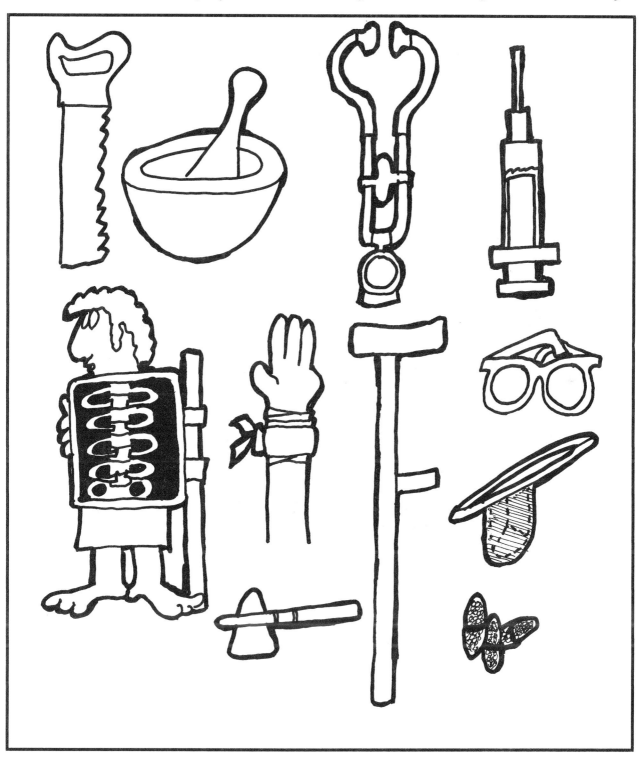

Tazria

Quotation

After seven days
the Kohein shall look at him.
If the rash is lighter
and has not spread
the Kohein shall say,
"He is clean."
The person shall wash his clothes
and be clean.

Leviticus 13.6

Discuss
Does believing help a sick person get better?

My Comment

Being sick is not much fun. The worst thing about being
sick is _____ .

Metzora מצרע

God teaches Aaron and his sons more about leprosy. Leprosy is a disease which can be caught by touching a person who has it. It is important to keep people with leprosy away from others. God shows the Kohanim how to help the lepers while keeping other people safe. Rules are given about how to know when the leprosy has been cured and when it is safe for them to came back to the camp.

God also teaches Aaron and his sons how to fix a house which has stuff oozing from the walls. God calls it "house leprosy."

Part of being a Kohein is taking care of other people.

Metzora

The Sick House

Have you ever seen a sick house? *Clean up this house by drawing it again without the slime.*

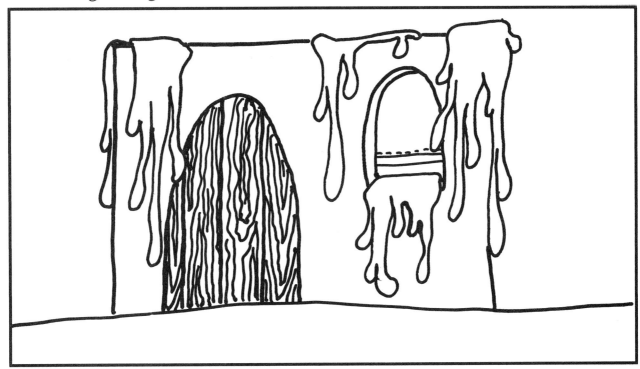

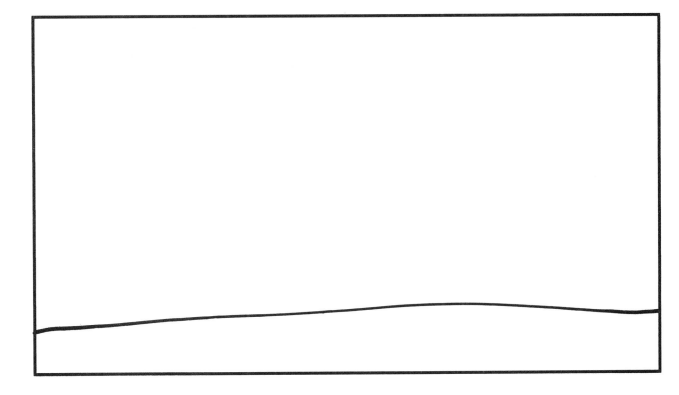

Quotation

When the Kohein comes in
and sees that the slime has not spread
after the house was plastered,
then the Kohein can announce
that the house is cured.

Leviticus 14.48

Discuss
When is a house well and when is a house sick?

My Comment

Even houses can get sick if no one takes care of them.
One way I can help take care of my house is
by _____ .

The Working Kohein

The Kohanim had many special jobs to do. *Next to each sentence, write the number of the picture which shows what the priest is doing.*

☐ Taking care of the always-burning light.

☐ Polishing the Menorah.

☐ Helping a mother with a new baby.

☐ Making the cakes (like pizza) which are given as gift-offerings to God

☐ Checking people who are sick.

☐ Cooking the Peace-offering.

Discuss
God wants the Jewish people to be a nation of kohanim and a holy people. How can we be like the kohanim?

Aharei Mot

אחרי מות

The most important day in the Jewish year is **Yom Kippur**. On Yom Kippur the Kohanim have to do very special things. The worship services on Yom Kippur are very special. God teaches Aaron and his sons all the things they will have to do to help the Jewish people ask for forgiveness.

God teaches that Yom Kippur is to be like a **special Shabbat**. No one is to work. All Jews are to spend the day making up for the bad things they have done in the past year.

God then lists some of the bad things that Jews should be very careful not to do.

Yom Kippur is different from every other day of the year. *Put an* X *through the things which we do not do on Yom Kippur.*

Praying in Synagogue

Eating a big turkey lunch

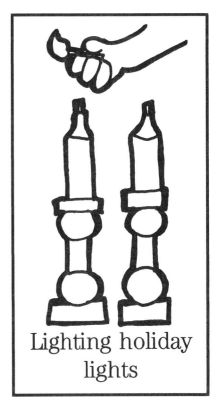

Lighting holiday lights

Playing dreidle

Saying, "I'm sorry."

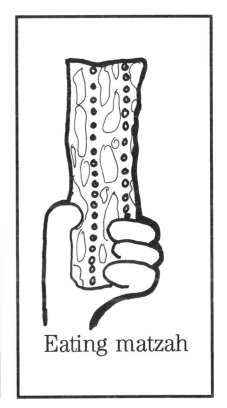

Eating matzah

Aharei Mot

Quotation

This shall be an everlasting law—
Once a year
the People of Israel shall make atonement
for all their sins.

Leviticus 16.34

Discuss
What does it mean "to make atonement?"

My Comment

Yom Kippur is the day when we try to become the best possible person we can be. One way I could become a better person is _____ .

Kedoshim

קדשים

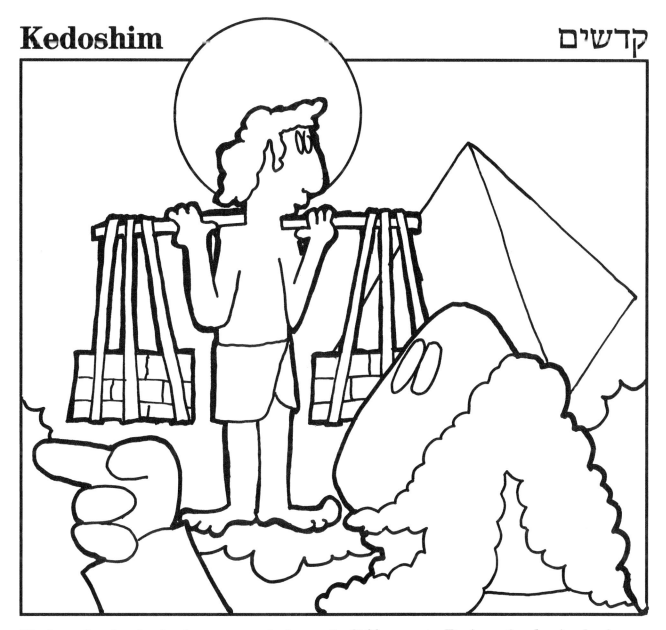

Being **holy** is being special and different. Being holy is being like God. God teaches all of the Jewish people, "**You should be holy because I, the Lord your God, am holy.**

God teaches that being holy is **honoring parents,** not worshiping idols, observing Shabbat, leaving the corners of your fields for those who are hungry, not stealing, not taking advantage of handicaps, judging cases fairly, not hating people, and loving your neighbor as yourself.

God reminds us to treat strangers fairly, because **we were strangers in the land of Egypt.**

Being Holy

God wants the Jewish people to be holy. *Cross out the pictures of things which are not holy.*

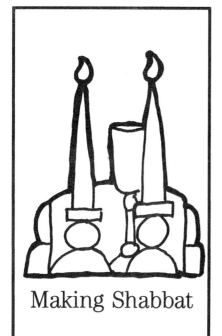

Making Shabbat

Helping Mother

Hitting a home run

Giving Tzedakah

Tripping a blind person

Stealing

Discuss
Is hitting a home run a holy thing to do?

110

The Hebrew root-word for "holy" is "Kodesh". It is spelled with 3 Hebrew letters.

Color the **Kuf** *red.*
Color the **Dalet** *blue.*
Color the **Shin** *yellow.*

Shin   Dalet   Kuf

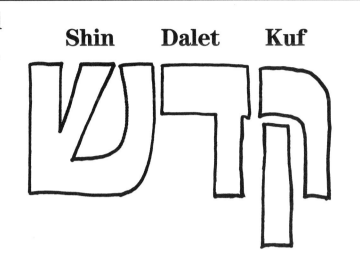

This sidrah is called **Kedoshim.** *Find the same three Hebrew letters.*

Color the **Kuf** *red.*
Color the **Dalet** *blue.*
Color the **Shin** *yellow.*

Mem   Yud   Shin   Dalet   Kuf

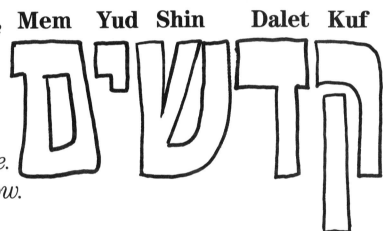

On Shabbat when we bless the wine, we make **Kiddush.** *Find the same three Hebrew letters.*

Color the **Kuf** *red.*
Color the **Dalet** *blue.*
Color the **Shin** *yellow.*

Shin   Vav   Dalet   Kuf

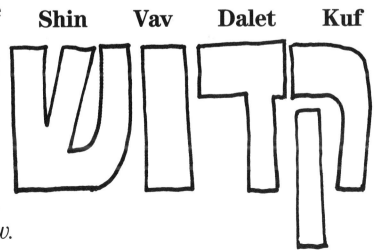

111

Kedoshim

Quotation

You shall be holy
for I the Lord your God am holy.

Leviticus 19.2

My Comment

We have many chances to be holy every day. One way I will
try to be holy is _____ .

Emor

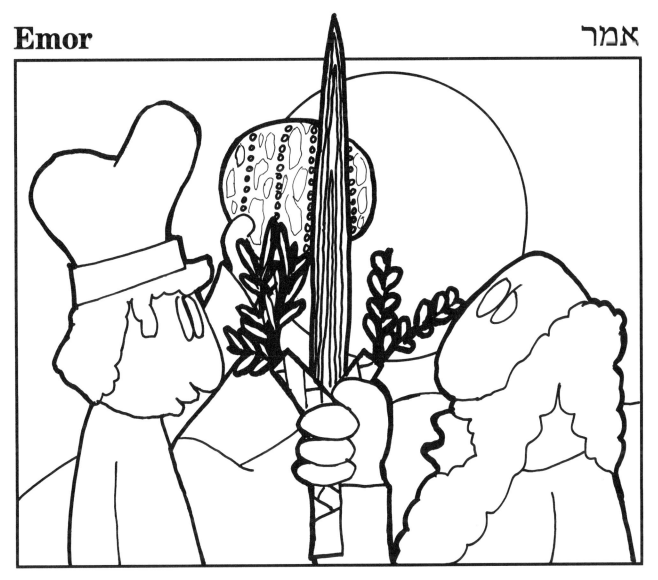

All Kohanim come from Aaron's family. They must come from the Kohein family of the Tribe of Levi. Levi was one of Israel's twelve sons. God teaches Moses more rules which help Aaron and his sons keep their family holy.

While Kohanim have special things to do every day, they do their most important work on holidays. God teaches Moses about **Shabbat**, **Passover**, **Shavuot** and **Sukkot**. Shabbat is a holiday which comes every week. We rest after a week of work because God rested after six days of creating. Passover, Shavuot and Sukkot are all harvest holidays. They are times that people bring gift-offerings to thank God for the good harvest.

Harvest Time

On Sukkot, Passover and Shavuot, farmers brought gift-offerings to the Temple in Jerusalem. Help this farmer find the right road to Jerusalem. *Draw the way he should take his gift-offerings.*

Holidays

This sidrah tells about many important Jewish holidays. Name these holidays. *Fill in the missing letters in the names in this crossword puzzle.*

1. The Seventh Day
2. Feast of Matzah
3. Festival of First Fruit
4. Day for Blowing the Shofar
5. Day of Atonement
6. Festival of Booths

SHABBAT
YOM KIPPUR
SUKKOT
SHAVUOT
ROSH HA-SHANAH
PASSOVER

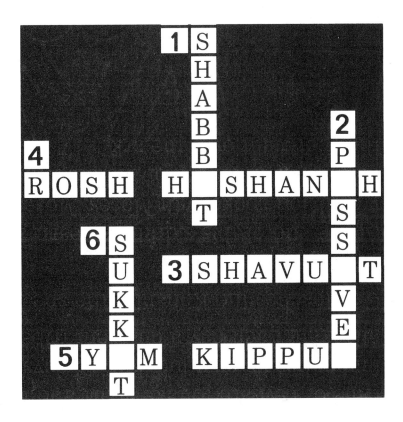

Quotation

These are the LORD's holidays,
holy gathering times,
which you should celebrate
at their right time of year.

Leviticus 23.4

Discuss
What are holidays for? Why do we have holidays? Jewish holidays?

My Comment

In this sidrah, we learn about many Jewish holidays. My favorite Jewish holiday is _____.

Be-har

בהר

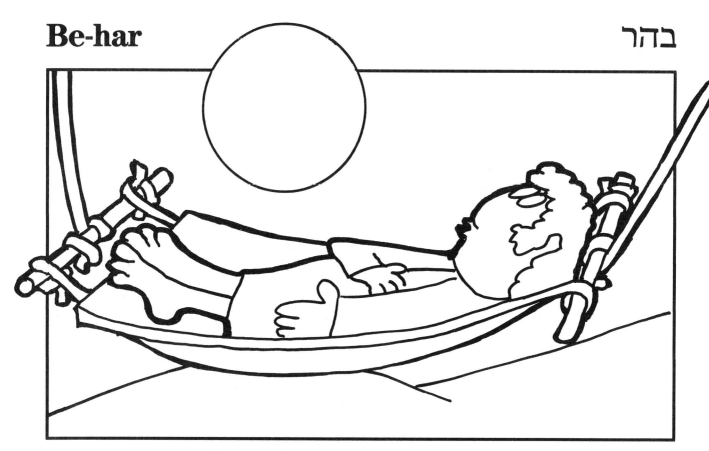

Most holidays last a day. Some holidays, like Sukkot and Passover, last for a whole week. This time, God teaches Moses the rules for two holidays which each last a whole year.

Shabbat comes once every seven days. We rest on every Shabbat. God teaches Moses that every seven years there is to be a "**Shabbat Year.**" In the seventh year, the land should get to rest. During a "Shabbat Year," Jews do **no farming**.

7 + 7 + 7 + 7 + 7 + 7 + 7 = 49. If you add 7 together seven times, it comes to 49. 50 is the number after 49. The year after the seventh "Shabbat Year" is called a"**Jubilee Year.**" It, too, is a year-long holiday. In a Jubilee Year, **everyone goes free**. In a Jubilee Year. we forget about any money which a person owes. In a Jubilee year, we blow the shofar and say "**Proclaim liberty throughout the land, to all the inhabitants thereof.**" These same words are written on the American Liberty Bell.

Every 7th year is called a "Shabbat-Year." *Color every 7th square on this number board blue.*

1	2	3	4	5	6	7	8	9	10
11	12	13	14	15	16	17	18	19	20
21	22	23	24	25	26	27	28	29	30
31	32	33	34	35	36	37	38	39	40
41	42	43	44	45	46	47	48	49	50
51	52	53	54	55	56	57	58	59	60
61	62	63	64	65	66	67	68	69	70
71	72	73	74	75	76	77	78	79	80
81	82	83	84	85	86	87	88	89	90
91	92	93	94	95	96	97	98	99	100

Find the square after the seventh blue square and color it Yellow. This is the "Jubilee-square."
Count another seven blue squares.
Color the second "Jubilee-square" yellow, too.

117

Be-har

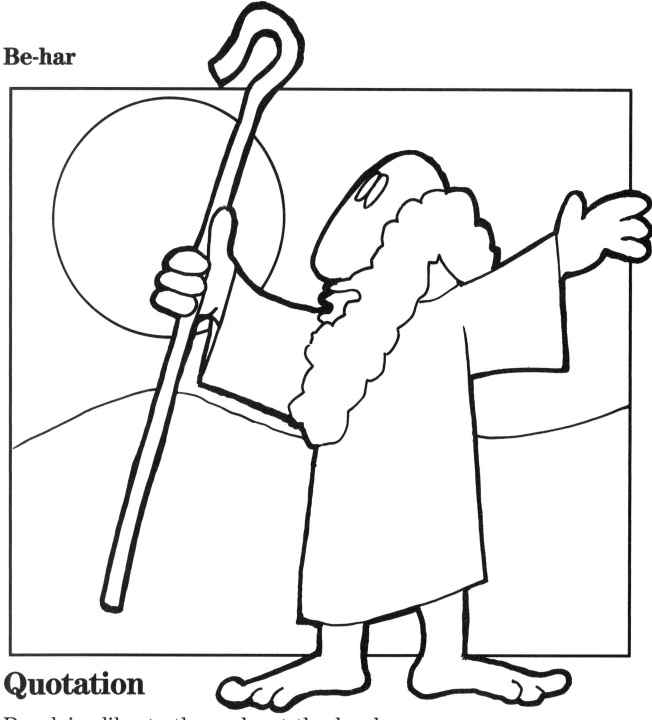

Quotation

Proclaim liberty throughout the land
to all the inhabitants thereof.

Leviticus 25.9

Discuss
Why did the founding-parents of the United States use a sentence from the Torah to mark
the Liberty Bell?

My Comment

This sentence from this sidrah is written on the Liberty Bell.
It reminds me that freedom is ＿＿＿＿＿＿＿＿＿＿ .

Beḥukotai

בחקתי

God has had Moses teach the Jewish people many laws and rules. God wants the Jewish people to follow these laws very carefully. Now God promises Israel's family **five blessings** if they obey all these teachings. God promises that these laws will make the Land of Israel into a place where much food grows and that following these laws will bring peace to that land. God explains that if they follow these laws they will not have to be afraid of having enemies and that the family will grow and be happy. Finally, God promises that if Israel's family keeps all the laws, God will be with them. God says, "I **will be your God and you will be My people."**

Then God warns that not following these rules will lead to very bad things.

Beḥukotai

This is the last sidrah in the book of Va-yikra. This book contains many mitzvot which teach us the right things to do. *Cross out those things which are not the right thing to do.*

Honor your parents

Fight with your parents

Pick on a person who is different

Be kind when someone needs help

Never take time to rest

Make Shabbat a special day

There are sentences in the Torah that are so important that it is good to memorize them. *Find the missing words. Then see if you can learn these three sentences by heart. Have someone test you.*

> You shall be ____ because I the LORD your God am holy.
>
> ____ your neighbor as yourself.
>
> Proclaim ____ throughout the land.
>
> | **love** | **liberty** | **holy** |

Discuss
Why is it important to learn some things by heart?

Quotation

These are the mitzvot
which the LORD commanded Moses
to teach the children of Israel
at Mt. Sinai.

Leviticus 27.34

My Comment

The book of Va-yikra is full of laws and rules. I think the most important rule to remember is _____.

Ḥazak Ḥazak V'Nitḥazeik

Almost no one reads a telephone book for fun. Still, a telephone book can teach us many important things. This sidrah is like a biblical telephone book. It tells us the names and numbers of Israel's family. Just like a phone book, it also tells us where they live.

Jacob's other name was Israel. He had 12 sons. Each of those sons had children. The family grew and grew. Each of the son's families became a tribe. The nation of Israel is made up of **12 tribes**.

God orders Moses to count all of the members of Israel's family who have lived longer than twenty years. **God names one leader in each tribe** to help. With their help, Aaron and Moses make a list of the whole Jewish people.

Then, God gives Moses a map of how the camp should look. The Mishkan is to be in the middle. Each tribe is to have its own place to camp around it.

In order to count the people, Moses had to know what tribe they came from. *Sort these people into tribes.*

1. All members of the tribe of Judah are tall and have curly hair. *Color their robes blue.*
   How many did you find? _____
2. All members of the tribe of Benjamin are short and have freckles. *Color their robes red.*
   How many did you find? _____

My Comment

If I had my own tribe, on my flag there would be

a _____ .

Map of the Tribes

	Asher	Dan

Benjamin		

Ephraim		The Mishkan

Manasseh		

	Gad	Reuben

Each tribe had its own special place around the Mishkan. Each tribe had its own flag to show where they should camp. Each flag had its own symbol. *Cut out the flags and glue them in the right places.*

Naphtali

Issachar

Levi

Judah

Zebulun

Simeon

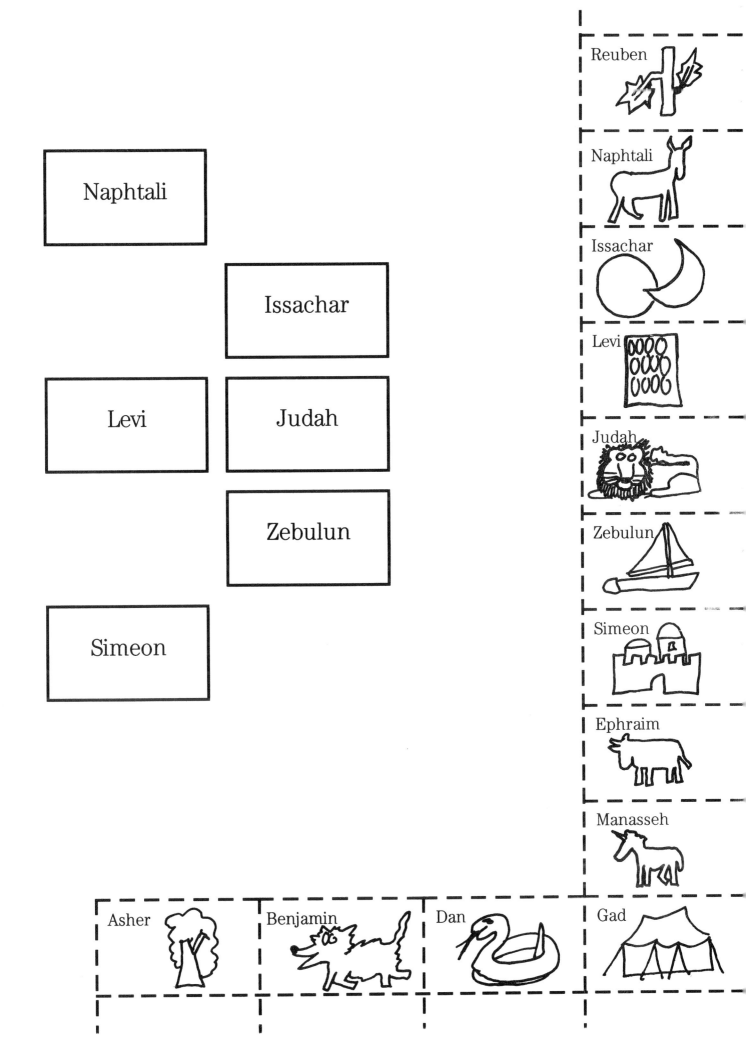

Reuben

Naphtali

Issachar

Levi

Judah

Zebulun

Simeon

Ephraim

Manasseh

Asher

Benjamin

Dan

Gad

Naso נשא

The nation of Israel camped at Mt. Sinai for a long time. They heard the Ten Commandments and were taught many laws. They built the Mishkan and learned all about the job of being a Kohein. God taught that the Kohanim were to be holy—and that all of Israel's family were also to be holy.

Now the Jewish people are ready to move. God teaches that tribe of Levi are to take apart and move the Mishkan. Each family has its own job. For 12 days gifts are brought to the Mishkan. Each day a different tribe brings gifts.

God teaches the Kohanim the special words to use to bless the Jewish people.

At the end of this sidrah we learn a secret. The secret is that when God spoke with Moses, Moses would hear a voice coming from on top of the covering. It would always be in the spot right over the ark.

Gifts

Here is the list of gifts that each tribe brought to the Mishkan. *Color in the right number of objects.*

1 Silver Bowl	6 Rams
1 Silver Basin	6 Lambs
1 Gold ladle	6 Goats
1 Bull	2 Oxen

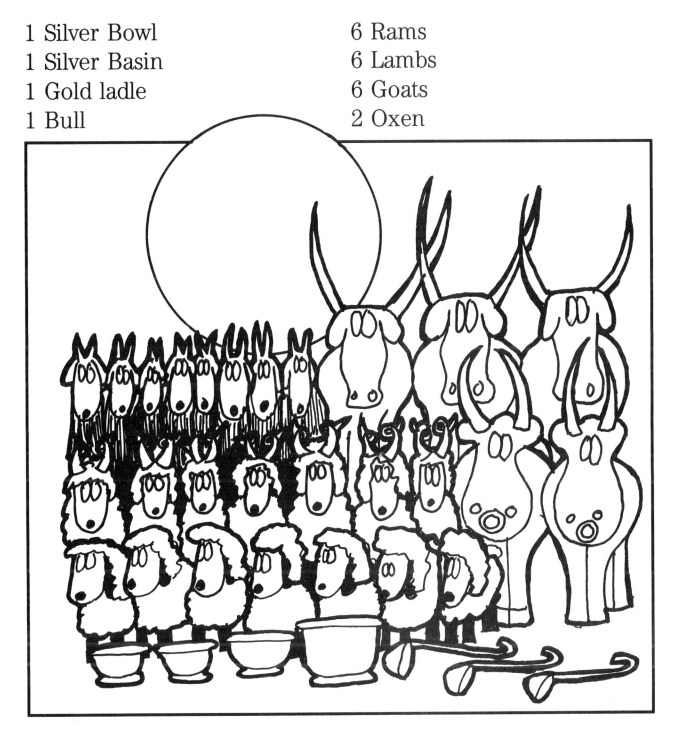

How many things did you color? _____

Naso

A Blessing

In Torah times the Head Kohein would use these words to bless the Jewish people. Today, parents use these words to bless their children on Shabbat.

יברכך יי וישמרך:
יאר יי פניו אליך ויחנך:
ישא יי פניו אליך. וישם לך שלום:

Y'varekh'kha Adonai v'yishm'rekha.
Ya'er Adonai panav elekha vihuneka.
Yisa Adonai panav elekha v'yasem l'kha shalom.

Discuss:
How can a parent bless a child?

QUOTATION

May the Lord bless you and protect you.
May the Lord's face shine on you and make things wonderful for you.
May the Lord's face turn towards you and give you peace.

Numbers 6.24-26

MY COMMENT

Parents use these words to bless their children. If I could write a blessing for my parents, I would ask God to bless them with_____.

Beha'alotekha

בהעלתך

The nation of Israel is almost ready to move. A good teacher goes over every lesson until every student understands. God repeats some teachings. God reviews the plans for the Menorah, the job of the tribe of Levi to help the Kohanim, and laws for Passover.

God then asks Moses to make **two silver horns** to call the people. When these are ready, God tells the tribes where to stand in the line. The people are now ready to move. **The ark is at the front of the line.**

Once again the people complain about the food. They want to have fish, cucumbers, melons, onions and garlic. These were the foods they ate in Egypt. Even though they have the special food manna, they want meat. Moses is angry at the people. God sends them a flock of birds to capture and eat.

129

Should the Blasts Be Long or Short?

God teaches Aaron's sons how to blow the silver horns. When it is time for the people to move, they should blow short blasts. When it is time for the people to come together, they should blow long blasts. *Look at these two pictures. Write down whether the horn blasts were long or short.*

Help to Carry the Ark

The ark was very heavy, but it was a special honor to carry it. *Finish this picture. Draw yourself carrying one side of the ark.*

Discuss
Carrying the ark was a hard job, but one which gave a person much honor. What are some hard things to do that can bring us honor?

QUOTATION

When the Ark was ready to move, Moses would say:
"Move forward, Lord!
Let your enemies be scattered
And let your foes run away
from You."

Numbers 10.35

MY COMMENT

These are the words we say when we take the Torah out of the ark. When I see the Torah, it makes me think of _____ .

Shelaḥ Lekha

שלח לך

God tells Moses to **send** twelve **spies into the land of Canaan**. God picks the leader of each tribe to go. Joshua is one of the spies. They spend 40 days scouting out the land. When they come back they are carrying a giant bunch of grapes. They tell the people that Canaan is **a land flowing with milk and honey**. They also tell them that the people who live in Canaan are giants. The spies are scared.

The People of Israel are scared too. Again they complain. They say, "We want to go back to Egypt." Joshua was the one spy who believed in God. He said, **"If the Lord is happy with us, we will have that land."** God is very angry with the people. Moses asks God to forgive the people. In the end the people are ready to enter the land. God then teaches some new rules to be taught to the people. These rules are all about how to live when they have their own land. The rule to **make fringes on the corner of a tallit** is the last rule.

Find the Hidden Spies

The spies sneaked into the Land of Israel. They came and went in secret. *Find the spies hiding in this picture.*

Things to Help us Remember

The Jewish people have many special things which help us remember our history, our mitzvot, and our special covenant with God. *Write the number of the picture in front of the thing it helps us remember.*

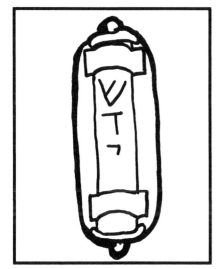

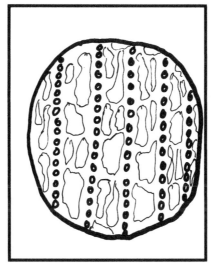

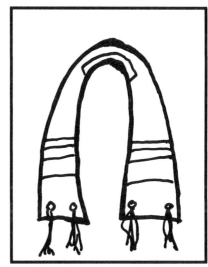

| 1. Mezuzah | 2. Matzah | 3. Tallit |

☐ God protected the houses of the Jews in Egypt.

☐ God taught many mitzvot to the People of Israel.

☐ The Jews had to leave Egypt in a hurry.

Discuss
What are some important things for Jews to remember?

QUOTATION

If the Lord is happy with us,
the Lord will bring us into this land—
a land that flows with milk and honey.

Numbers 14.8

MY COMMENT

Joshua thought of the Land of Israel as "a land flowing with milk and honey." I think of Israel as_____ .

Korah  קרח

Korah is a member of the tribe of Levi. He doesn't think that it is fair that Moses and Aaron are the bosses. He says that all Jews are holy and that no one person should be in charge. Korah wants to be the boss of the Mishkan instead of Aaron. Some people are on his side. Moses says, "God will pick." Then the earth opens up and swallows Korah and the people on his side. They are gone.

Many of the people are angry that Korah and his friends are dead. They yell at Moses and Aaron. God tells Moses what to do. Moses asks the leader of each tribe to write his name on his staff and put it in the Mishkan. Aaron does the same thing. The next day, Aaron's staff turns into a tree. It has leaves, flowers, and almonds. This is a sign that God has picked Aaron and his family.

God then teaches more about what a Kohein does. When Israel moves into Canaan, the tribe of Levi will be given no land. Instead, they will work for God. God teaches a rule: all Jewish farmers must share part of their harvest with the tribe of Levi.

The Fall of Korah

Not every story in the Torah is a happy one. In this story, Korah tries to become the boss. God has to stop him. God opens a hole in the ground which swallows him and his followers. *Connect the dots to show this pit. Color it black.*

Koraḥ

Aaron's Staff

There are two stories in the Torah where Aaron's staff changes into something else. When Moses and Aaron first went to Pharaoh, Aaron's staff became a snake. In this story it turned into a tree with flowers and almonds.

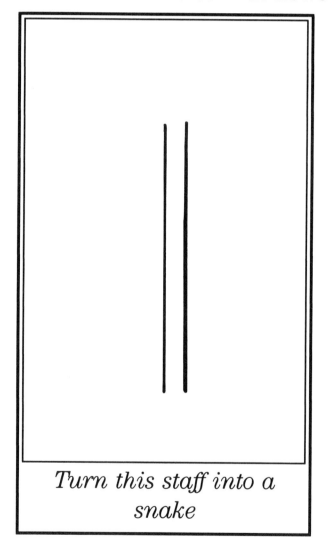

Turn this staff into a snake

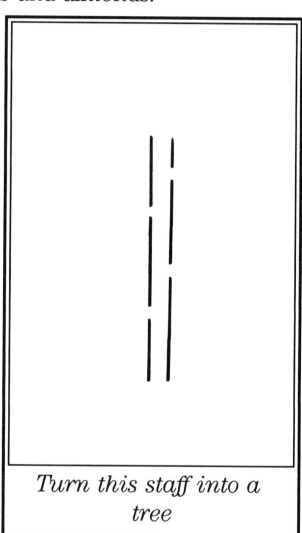

Turn this staff into a tree

MY COMMENT

Koraḥ and his followers didn't understand that God picked Moses and Aaron to be leaders because they were the best people for the job. One thing I don't understand about God is ＿＿＿＿＿＿＿＿＿＿＿＿＿＿＿ .

Ḥukkat

RED

God teaches still more about the Head Kohein's job. The instructions are given for a special offering made with an **all-red cow**. Also among the teachings are some rules about what to do when a person dies.

Miriam is Moses' sister. She dies and is buried at Kadesh. Yet again, the people complain. Again they want water. Again they want to go back to Egypt. This time God tells Moses to **take his staff and talk to a rock**. The people yell. **Moses takes the staff and hits the rock.** God is angry. God tells **Moses** that he **will not lead the Jewish people into the Land which will become Israel**.

The people of Israel want to walk through the country of Edom. Their king says no. Edom has a very strong army. The people of Israel walk another way. Aaron dies and his son Eliezar becomes the Head Kohein. The King of Arad tries to stop Israel with his army, but Israel wins. Israel's family wants to walk through the country of the Amorites. The King of the Amorites tries to stop them. Again, Israel wins. They also beat the King of Bashan.

Brothers and Sisters

Moses and his brother and sister were a very important family in Jewish history. *Connect these important brothers and sisters by drawing lines.*

Joseph

Rachel

Miriam

Jacob

Leah

Aaron

Esau

Benjamin

Moses

Discuss
Even though God always helped them find water, the people of Israel are always afraid that they will have no water. They were afraid with no real reason. When are you afraid with no real reason?

QUOTATION

The people said to Moses, "Why did you make us leave Egypt and bring us to this horrible place—a place with no grain or figs or vines or pomegranates? There is not even water to drink."

Numbers 20.5

MY COMMENT

Some people always find things to complain about! One thing I complain about too much is _____ _____

Balak

בלק

Balak is the King of Moab. He is scared of the Nation of Israel. He knows what they did to the Amorites and the others. He hires **Balaam**. Balaam is a soothsayer. Balaam promises to stop Israel's family with a curse.

Balaam picks a mountain as the place to say the curse. He rides a donkey to the place. Three times God makes the donkey go the wrong way. Balaam is angry. He yells at the donkey. God makes the donkey yell back. God then tells Balaam that he will **bless Israel and not curse them**.

When Balaam looks down on Israel's camp, he blesses them: **"Your tents are beautiful, Jacob. So is your Mishkan, Israel."**

The Way to the Top

Help Balaam's donkey find the right way up the mountain.
Draw the way he should go.

Balak

Balaam's donkey yells back at Balaam when he is not fair. What would these animals say if they could talk?

Discuss

Balaam is a person who totally changed his mind. He went to curse Israel and wound up blessing them. When was one time you totally changed your mind?

QUOTATION

Your tents are beautiful, Jacob.
So is your Mishkan, Israel.

Numbers 24.5

MY COMMENT

When Balaam saw the place where the Jewish people worshipped, he said these words. When we, the Jewish people, get together to pray today, we begin with these words. When Jews get together to pray, one beautiful thing is _____ .

Pinḥas

פינחס

Pinḥas is one Aaron's sons. He teaches Israel's family that some things are wrong. God blesses him. Again, God asks Moses to count the number of people in Israel's family. Eliezar, another son of Aaron, helps him.

After the counting, God explains that each man will be given a piece of the Promised Land for his family. Two women complain. They say, "We are the daughters of Zelopheḥad. Our father is dead. We have no brothers. Our family should have a piece of land, too." God agrees.

God asks Moses to climb to the top of a hill. God shows him the Promised Land. God reminds him that he will not cross into the land of Canaan. God tells him to make **Joshua** the next leader of Israel's family. God reminds Moses about Shabbat, Pesaḥ, Shavuot, Rosh Ha-Shanah, Yom Kippur and Sukkot.

Jewish Women

This sidrah reminds us that women are important members of every family. Here is a review of some of the important women in the Torah. *Write the number of the correct picture next to each sentence.*

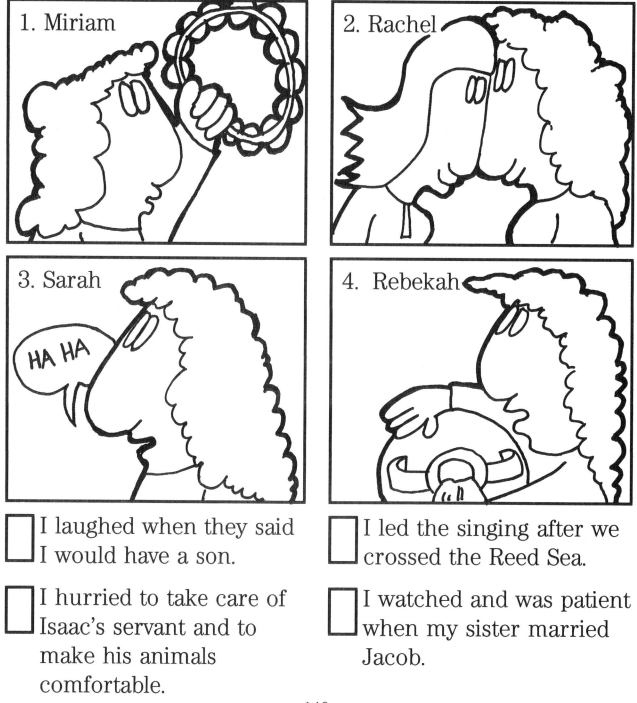

1. Miriam
2. Rachel
3. Sarah
4. Rebekah

☐ I laughed when they said I would have a son.

☐ I hurried to take care of Isaac's servant and to make his animals comfortable.

☐ I led the singing after we crossed the Reed Sea.

☐ I watched and was patient when my sister married Jacob.

The Leaders

Joshua is going to be the next leader of Israel's family.
Number these leaders in order.

☐ Moses   ☐ Jacob   ☐ Abraham

☐ Joshua   ☐ Joseph   ☐ Isaac

Discuss
How would you like to be like each of these famous Jews?

QUOTATION

Pick Joshua, the son of Nun,
a man who has spirit in him,
and lay your hand upon him.

Numbers 27.18

MY COMMENT

If I had to pick a leader, I would look for a person
who _____ .

Mattot

The nation of Israel goes to war with the Midianites. They win that war.

Israel's family camps just across the Jordan river from the land of Canaan. The tribe of **Reuben** and the tribe of **Gad** come to Moses. They ask if they can have land on this side of the Jordan river. Moses is angry. He says: "**Do you want to stay here while your brothers go to war to take the land God promised to Abraham, Isaac and Jacob?**" They answered him, "**We will go and fight alongside you. Then we will come back to this side of the river.**" Moses says, "**If you keep this promise, God will give your families this land.**"

Good for the Animals

The tribes of Reuben and Gad wanted to stay on the far side of the Jordan river because the land there was good for their cattle.

Match the animal with the place which would be the best place for it to live.

Mattot

Desert Life

Israel's family spent 40 years in the desert. *Put a ✓ (check) next to the sentences which tell what it was like in the desert.*

_____There was plenty of water to drink.
_____There was very little water to drink.

_____There were lots of different kinds of foods.
_____God provided manna and birds for people to eat.

_____The people were all friendly to Israel.
_____Sometimes Israel's family had to fight wars.

Discuss
What was it like to spend 40 years in the desert?

QUOTATION

The tribes of Reuben and Gad said:
"We will not return to our homes
until every one of Israel's families
are living on their land."

Numbers 32.18

MY COMMENT

The tribes of Reuben and Gad had to go ahead and help the other tribes even though they wanted to stay on their own land. One time I helped someone when I wanted to do something else, was when_____ .

Masei

מסעי

Israel's family is almost ready to enter the land of Canaan.
The Torah tells about all the places they have been since
they left Egypt. God teaches them more about living in the
Promised Land.

God has Moses teach the people about the borders of the
Land of Israel. Moses describes the part of the land which
will be given to each family. Then God teaches Moses more
rules which will help the people to live together in peace.

Masei

Follow Israel's Journey

This is the last sidrah in the book of Bamidbar. It shows us how Israel's family traveled to many places in the wilderness and had many adventures. *Follow the directions to lead Israel's family out of Egypt and to the edge of the Jordan.*

1. The Israelites started out from **Rameses**.
2. They went to **Sukkot** where there were palm trees.
3. They camped by the **Sea of Reeds**.
4. They went to **Rephidim** where there was no water.
5. They went to **Sinai**.
6. They camped out at **Mount Hor**, where Aaron died.
7. They stopped by the **Jordan River** near Jericho.

Discuss
What was the hardest part of spending forty years in the wilderness?

QUOTATION

This is the story of Israel's travels
who started out in Egypt, group by group—
led by Moses and Aaron.

Numbers 33.1

MY COMMENT

Israel spent forty years in the wilderness and had many adventures. I think the most exciting part was _____ _____ .

152

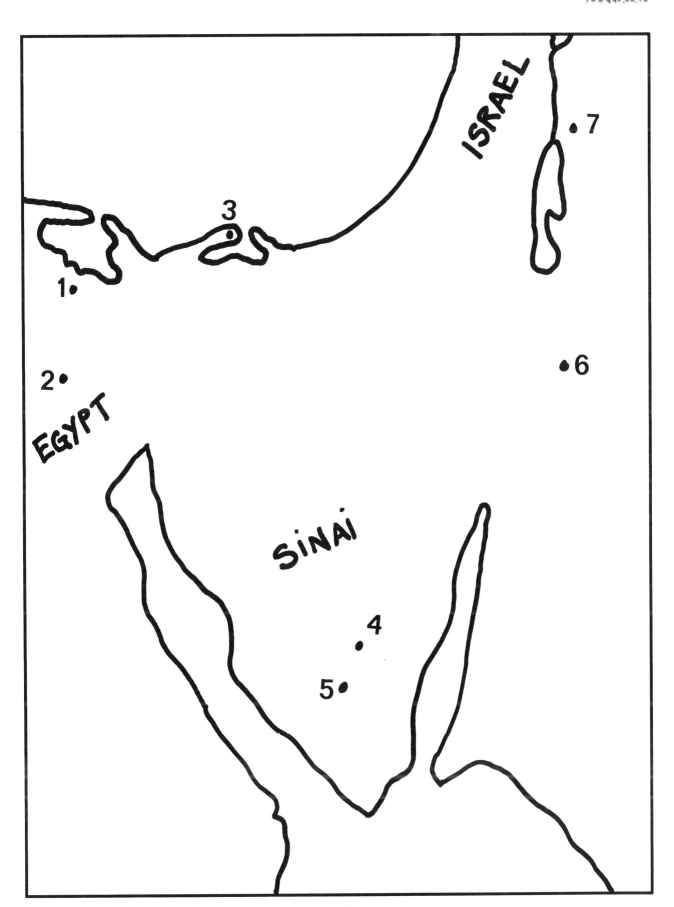

Devarim

דברים

Israel is camped **across the river** from the Promised Land. God has said that Moses cannot cross. Forty years have passed since Israel's family left Egypt. All the people who left Egypt except for Moses and Joshua have died. Everyone else was born in the wilderness. Moses gathers the people of Israel for his final lessons.

Moses begins with history. He reminds them of all the times **they complained and made God angry**. He reviews the wars they have fought and won. He also reminds the tribes of **Gad** and **Reuben** that they **promised to fight alongside their brothers**. Moses again tells the people that **Joshua will be their leader**, and that **God will help them win the land**.

Devarim Means Words

Devarim is the last book of the Torah. The Hebrew word *Devarim* means "words." *Find these words in this puzzle.*

Torah	Yom Kippur
Shabbat	Passover
Moses	Mishkan
Israel	Mitzvah

```
X X X X X X X M I S H K A N X
X X X P X X X I X X X X X X X
X S H A B B A T X X X X I X X
X X X S X X X Z X X X X S X X
X M O S E S X V X X X X R X X
X X X O X X X A X X X A X X X
X X X V X X X H X X X E X X X
X X X E X X X X X X X L X X X
X X X R X X X X X X X X X X X
X X X X X X X X X X T X X X
X X X X X X X X X X O X X X
X X Y O M X K I P P U R X X X
X X X X X X X X X X A X X X
X X X X X X X X X X H X X X
X X X X X X X X X X X X X X X
```

Can you tell why each of these words is important?

Our Family History

Moses helps Israel's family remember their history. *Number the sentences in the order they happened.*

_____ Israel spends forty years in the wilderness.

_____ Jacob wrestles with an angel. His name is changed to Israel.

_____ Moses leads Israel's family out of slavery in Egypt.

_____ God makes two promises to Abraham: a large family and the land of Israel.

_____ God teaches Moses the Ten Commandments and other Mitzvot.

_____ Joseph runs Egypt. He brings his family to Egypt.

Discuss
Why is it important to remember history?

QUOTATION

On the other side of the Jordan,
in the land of Moab,
Moses taught Torah.

Deuteronomy 1.5

MY COMMENT

In this sidrah Moses begins to reteach the Torah. I think the most important thing I've learned in the Torah so far

is _____ .

Va-ethannan

Moses goes on teaching. He tells the people how he begged God to let him go into the Promised Land. God said no. Moses then warns the people to be very careful to obey God's rules. He then repeats the **Ten Commandments**.

Moses warns the people not to worship the stars or idols but to remember the One God. He reminds them that they are a **holy people** and have a special friendship with God. God took them out of Egypt and gave them the Torah. It is very important to follow the Torah's rules.

The Ten Commandments

The Ten Commandments are so important that they are written two times in the Torah. *Match the commandment and the picture.*

☐ No Idols

☐ Keep Shabbat

☐ Honor Parents

☐ No Murder

☐ No Stealing

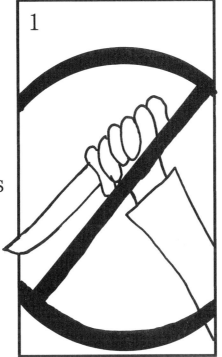

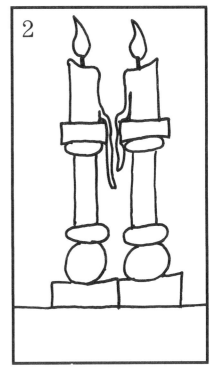

Va-eṭhannan

The Shema

In this sidrah we find one of the most important Jewish prayers. *Say the words in Hebrew and English. Color the Hebrew letters.*

שמע ישראל יי אלהינו יי אחד

Shema Yisra-el Adonai Eloheinu Adonai Eḥad.
Hear O Israel, the Lord our God, the Lord is One.

Discuss
Why do Jews say the Shema at night before going to sleep?

QUOTATION

You should love the Lord your God
with all your heart
with all your soul
and with all your might.

Deuteronomy 6.5

MY COMMENT

One way my family shows that we love God is

by _____ .

Ekev   עקב

Moses goes on with his final lessons. He goes over how important it is to follow God's rules. He says, "**Remember, the Lord your God is bringing you to a good land.** It is a land with streams and springs and lakes coming from the plains and hills. It is a land of wheat and barley, of vines, figs, and pomegranates, a land of olive oil and of honey."

Moses remembers going up Mt. Sinai and getting the Ten Commandments. He reminds the people that he had to make a second set of tablets. Over and over he reminds the people that **following the rules in the Torah will lead them to a good life.**

The Promised Land

The Promised Land was a beautiful place. *Finish this picture and fill it with beautiful colors.*

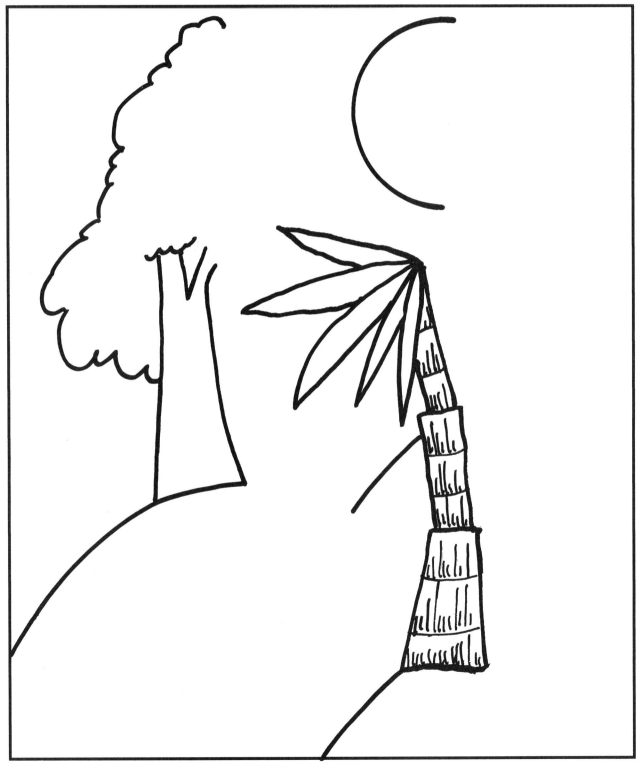

Remembering the Torah

It is important to remember the laws and lessons taught in the Torah. Many parts of our body help us to remember these rules. *Match the things which go together.*

Ear

Hands

Mouth

Eyes

reading the Torah

singing the Shema

holding the Torah

hearing a shofar

Discuss
What are some other ways of remembering to live by the Torah?

QUOTATION

Israel, what does the Lord your God want from you? To love your God and walk in God's path.

Deuteronomy 10.12

MY COMMENT

One way I can walk in God's path is by _____.

Re'eh ראה

Good

Evil

Moses explains that **everyone has a choice**. Every person must decide if he or she will do good or do bad. Choosing to do **good** and following the rules of the Torah will **bring a blessing**. We can also choose to do what is **wrong**. We can choose **the curse**.

Moses says that the people have to be very careful not to worship the gods of the people of Canaan. They must be true to the One real God. They must be different. He reminds the people of the rules about the kinds of food they can eat. He again teaches that they must share part of their harvest with the tribe of Levi. They must also **share part of their harvest** with those who need food. Moses reminds them that Israel's family must **take care of those who are in need**.

Again, Moses goes over the holidays of **Passover**, **Shavuot**, and **Sukkot**. These are times to thank God.

The Choice

God wants us to make the right choice. Each child on these pages must make a choice. *Draw the right way for each child to go.*

David has candy.

David eats all the candy.

David shares candy with his friend.

Cherie's little sister is crying.

Cherie yells at her sister.

Cherie asks her, "What is wrong?"

Re'eh

Michael finds George Smith's wallet.

Michael looks for Mr. Smith.

Michael keeps the money.

Jennifer is mad at her mother.

Jennifer yells at her mother.

Jenifer tells her mother, "I am angry."

Being Different—Being Special

Moses taught that Israel's family should not copy the ways of the people around them. They must be different. *Circle the things that make this Jewish home different from other homes.*

Discuss
How is a Jewish home different from other homes?

QUOTATION

Do not harden your hearts
and shut your hand against those in need.
You must open your hand
and lend them what they need.

Deuteronomy 15.7-8

MY COMMENT

My family helps those in need by _____ .

Shoftim

This time Moses starts by teaching about courts. He tells the people that they must pick judges and leaders. All judges must be fair. He says, **"Justice, you must seek Justice."**

Moses then teaches about kings. He says, "when you move into the land, you can pick a king if you want one." He then teaches that the king must write his own copy of the Torah and follow every law in it.

Moses then prepares the people to fight for the land. He gives them rules for fighting a just war. One rule is that they must try to **offer peace before they fight.** Another rule says that they cannot cut down fruit trees. **Even if it is the best way to take over a city, they cannot cut down trees which give food.**

Three Different Jewish Leaders

In this sidrah, Moses teaches about Jewish leaders. There have been many kinds of Jewish leaders. Follow the directions to learn about three of them.

Judge

Prophet

Moses taught the words of God to Israel's family.

* *Draw the tablets of the Ten Commandments in Moses' hands.*
* *Write his name on the line.*

Deborah showed the way to make fair decisions. She would sit under a palm tree and listen to people's problems.

* *Finish Deborah's palm tree.*
* *Write her name on the line.*

King

David ruled over the land of Israel. He also wrote and sang Psalms, songs which praised God.

* *Draw David's harp.*
* *Write his name on the line.*

Shoftim

Seeking Justice

Judges are important leaders. In this sidrah, Moses reminds the people that judges must be fair. The Hebrew word for justice is צדק **Tzedek.**

Color the צ **Tzadee** *red*
Color the ד **Dalet** *blue*
Color the ק **Kuf** *yellow.*

נמפזצדקרטאמשיכע

Can you find the word צדק in this line? *Circle it.*

A Rule About Trees

Even in war, Israel's family must follow rules. They must try to make peace. They may not cut down any fruit trees.

Draw the fruit on these trees. Color them alive and healthy.

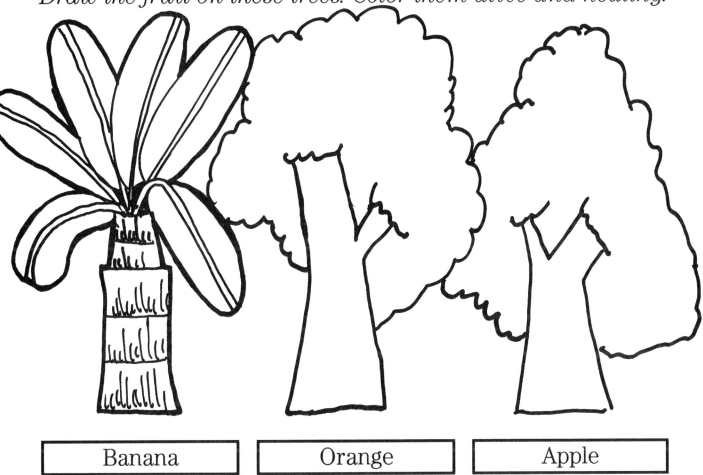

| Banana | Orange | Apple |

Discuss
How do rules help to make things fair? What makes a fair rule?

QUOTATION

Justice, you must seek justice.

Deuteronomy 16.20

MY COMMENT

People have to seek justice. They have to find the right things to do. One way I can seek justice is _____ .

171

Ki Tetze

Moses is still teaching. This time he begins by talking about the family. There are many rules: **Parents must be fair** to all their children. **Children must obey** their parents.

Then Moses talks about being a good neighbor. He teaches that **a person must return a sheep or ox which has gotten lost. A person must help a hurt animal. A person must put a wall around a flat roof** to keep people from falling off.

Finally, Moses talks about how one person should help another. It is a rule that if you **loan money and the person cannot pay it back, you must be kind to him.** You also must be fair to everyone who works for you. And, you must **leave part of your fields unharvested so that people who are hungry can come and gather the food that they need.**

Good Fences

The Torah teaches that a good Jew protects his or her neighbors from things which might hurt them. *Draw the right protection for each of these dangerous things.*

A Dog who Bites

A Flat Roof

An Open Fire

An Open Pit

Doing Justly

The Torah teaches us to be just to both animals and people.
Put an **A** *next to the rules about* **Animals**.
Put a **P** *next to the rules about* **People**.

____ Do not take both a mother bird and her eggs. Let the mother go.

____ Do not make an ox and a donkey plow together.

____ Let an animal eat when it is working in the field.

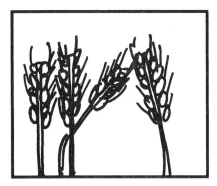

____ Leave some of the food in your field for the poor.

____ Pay the people who work for you on time.

____ Be honest in your business.

Discuss
What is just about each of these rules?

QUOTATION

The Lord your God hates it when one person cheats another.

Deuteronomy 25.16

MY COMMENT

One good way to make sure that no one cheats
is _____ .

Ki Tavo

כי תבוא

Moses is coming to the end of his long review lesson. He teaches the people that after they enter the Land which God is giving to them, they must give **their first fruits to God as a gift-offering**. When they give the offering, they should repeat the history of Israel, like this:

My father was a wandering Aramean. He went down to Egypt with a small family. He stayed there and became a great nation. The Egyptians hurt us, picked on us, and made us work for them. We cried to the LORD, the God of our parents. God heard our cry and saw us suffering. The LORD freed us from Egypt and brought us to this land, and gave it to us. It is a land flowing in milk and honey.

Then Moses reminds the people that God will curse those who break the Torah's rules and bless those who follow them.

175

Ki Tavo

The First Prayer

In this sidrah we find the oldest Jewish Prayer. It was said when the Jewish people brought gift-offerings. It tells their story.

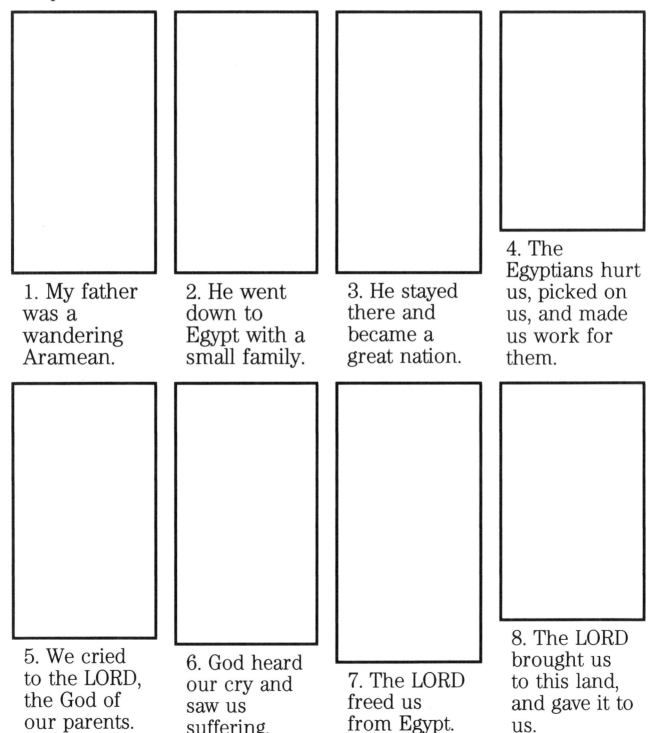

1. My father was a wandering Aramean.

2. He went down to Egypt with a small family.

3. He stayed there and became a great nation.

4. The Egyptians hurt us, picked on us, and made us work for them.

5. We cried to the LORD, the God of our parents.

6. God heard our cry and saw us suffering.

7. The LORD freed us from Egypt.

8. The LORD brought us to this land, and gave it to us.

Find the right top to each picture. Color it. Cut it out, and paste it in place.

Ki Tavo

First Fruits

Moses taught that the first fruits picked in the Promised Land were special. Do you remember these firsts? *Fill in the missing word.*

The First Day
On the first day God said, "Let there be _____ ."

The First People
Adam and Eve were the first people. God made them in God's _____ .

The First Jew
God said to Abraham "I will make your future-family as many as the _____ in the sky."

The First Commandment
The first commandment teaches, "I am the _____ your God."

Stars   LORD
Image   Light   What was your first word? _____ .

Ki Tavo

QUOTATION

Today you know for sure
that the LORD is your God...
And today the LORD knows for sure
that you are God's treasured people.

Deuteronomy 26.17-18

MY COMMENT

I feel part of a special people when_____.

Moses gathers together all of Israel's family. He tells them, "**You are standing here today, all of you, before the LORD your God**. Today, you will make a covenant with God. God will keep the promise made to Abraham, Isaac, and Jacob and you will become the **Chosen People**. This covenant is for everyone standing here today, and for all of the Jews who will be born in the future."

Moses teaches, "**The law is not too hard nor too difficult to understand**. It is not way up in the sky, nor far away across the see. The Torah is very close to you. It is in your mouth and in your heart."

Moses commands the people to "**choose life**, and follow the Torah."

Listening to Moses

When Moses said, "You are standing here, today before the LORD your God," he was talking to the Jews alive then and to all the Jewish people who would be born in the future. This means that Moses was talking to you, too. *Put yourself in this picture. Show the way you would listen to Moses.*

Moses also said, "The Torah is not in the sky. It is not across the sea." Moses said that we can find it in our mouth and in our heart. *Draw your mouth and your heart filled with Torah.*

In our lives we can choose to do good or we can choose to be bad. *Circle the pictures that show good choices. Cross out the choices that are bad.*

Fighting

Making Friends

Learning Torah

Scribbling on Books

Helping injured Animals

Hurting an Animal

Discuss
How can the Torah be in your heart and your mouth?

QUOTATION

Choose life by loving the LORD your God, keeping God's laws and following God's way.

Deuteronomy 30.20

MY COMMENT

I choose life when I choose to _____ .

183

Vayelekh

וילך

Moses is 120 years old. Soon he will die. Joshua will lead the Jewish people into the Promised land.

Moses finishes writing down all of his teachings. Moses gives all his teachings to the Kohanim. They put the writings in the ark.

God tells Joshua to be strong and not to give up. God says. "You will lead the Jewish people into the Promised Land. I will be with you."

Moses lived a long life and was a great leader. Here are some scenes from Moses' life. *Follow the directions to help finish "The Adventures of Moses."*

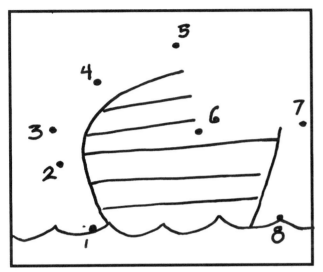

1. Moses is found in a basket. *Connect the dots to finish the basket.*

2. Moses sees the burning bush. *Draw the flames.*

3. Moses tells Pharaoh to let the Jews go. *Color the frogs green.*

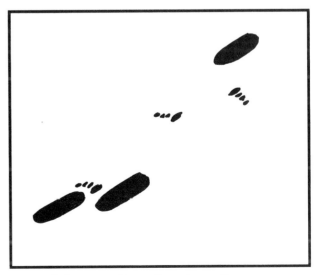

4. Moses leads the Jews across the Reed Sea. *Finish the footprints.*

Vayelekh

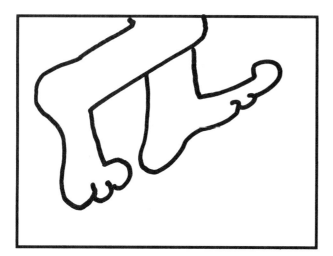

5. Moses goes up Mt. Sinai and gets the Ten Commandments. *Draw the mountain.*

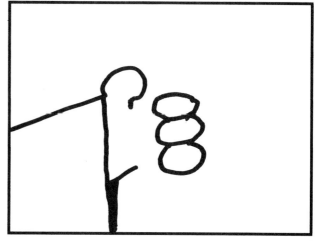

6. Moses leads the Jews though the wilderness. *Draw in Moses' staff.*

7. Moses tells Joshua to be strong and lead the Jewish people. *Write "Be Strong."*

Discuss
What made Moses the greatest leader of the Jewish people?

QUOTATION

Moses called Joshua and said to him before all of Israel:
"Be strong and brave
for it is you who will go with this people
into the Land which God promised to their parents..."

Deuteronomy 31.7

MY COMMENT

Moses told Joshua not to be afraid to be the new leader. A new thing which was scary for me to do was _____.

Ha'azinu

 האזינו

Moses recites a poem. The poem is all about God and Israel. God protects and takes care of Israel. Israel isn't always good. Even when Israel does wrong, God still protects them.

After the poem, Moses goes up to the top of **Mount Nebo**. From the top of this mountain, Moses can see the Promised Land. He can look at the land in the distance, but God will not let him go there.

Ha'azinu

The name of this sidrah means "Listen!". We listen to many special sounds during the Jewish year. *Write the correct number in the box with each picture.*

☐ Shofar

☐ Rimonim

☐ Gragger

☐ Matzah

1. I call you to "wake up" and pay attention on Rosh Ha-Shanah.
2. I jingle with happy sounds as you dance with the Torah on Simhat Torah.
3. I make so much noise that you cannot hear the name Haman on Purim.
4. I crunch in you mouth during Pesah.

Ha'azinu is a special because it is a poem, not a story. *Fill in the missing words to finish this poem.*

Children of Israel
Listen to me
Once you were slaves
Now you are _____.

For forty years
you have walked through the sand
Now you can enter
The promised _____.

Remember the laws.
Try to do what you should.
Try to be kind.
Try to be _____.

Wherever you go and
Whatever you do
Always be proud
That you are a _____.

Quotation

Remember the days of old,
Recall the years that have passed.
Ask you parents, they will explain it,
The older people, they will tell you.

Deuteronomy 32.7

Discuss:
What kinds of things can you learn from older people?

My Comment

One thing I learned from listening to my parents and grandparents was that _____.

V'zot Habrakhah

Moses blesses the family of Israel. He gives each tribe its own blessing. From the top of the mountain **God shows Moses the whole land of Israel.** He sees the place God promised to Abraham, Isaac, and Jacob.

Moses dies. God buries him. The people of Israel spend 30 days crying for Moses. Joshua becomes the new leader.

Moses was a special prophet. **No other Jewish leader will ever be able to do all the things which Moses did.**

At the end of his life, Moses had led the family of **Israel** to the land of **Israel**. The people now have a home.

Here is the Hebrew word *yisrael*, Israel. *Trace the letters in blue and color them in.*

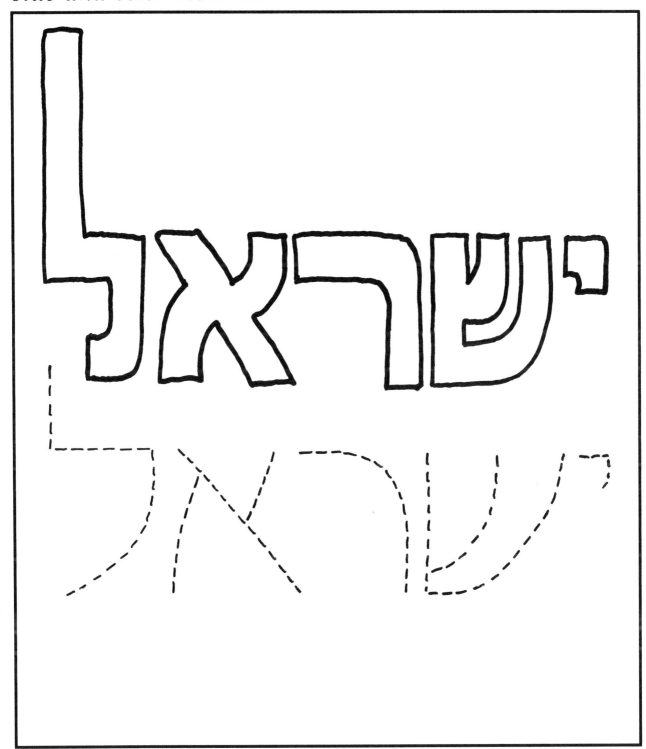

V'zot Habrakhah

This is the last sidrah in the Torah. As soon as we finish reading it, we begin the Torah all over again. The circle never ends. *Cut out the five pie-pieces. Place the five books of the Torah in the right order. Glue them in place.*

MY COMMENT

I think it is important to read the Torah over and over again because _____ .